Intellectuals In the Middle Ages

INTELLECTUALS IN THE MIDDLE AGES

Jacques Le Goff

Translated from the French by Teresa Lavender Fagan

BLACKWELL
Cambridge MA & Oxford UK

Copyright © Editions du Seuil, 1957; 1985
English translation © Basil Blackwell 1993

The right of Jacques Le Goff to be identified as author of this work has been
asserted in accordance with the Copyright, Designs and Patents Act 1988.

First published 1993

Blackwell Publishers
238 Main Street
Cambridge, Massachusetts 02142, USA

108 Cowley Road
Oxford OX4 1JF, UK

Library of Congress Cataloging-in-Publication Data
Le Goff, Jacques, 1924–
    [Intellectuels au Moyen Age.   English]
    Intellectuals in the Middle Ages / Jacques Le Goff : translated
from the French by Teresa Lavender Fagan.
        p.   cm.
    Includes bibliographical references and index.
    ISBN 0–631–17078–2 (hb.). — ISBN 0–631–18519–4 (pbk.)
    1. Civilization, Medieval.   2. Europe—Intellectual life.
    3. Learning and scholarship—History—Medieval, 500–1500.
    I. Title.
    CB351.L41513   1992
    940.1—dc20   92–27155
                                                          CIP
British Library Cataloguing in Publication Data
A CIP catalogue record for this book is available from the British Library.

Typeset in 10½ on 13 pt Baskerville
by TecSet Ltd, Wallington, Surrey
Printed in the United States of America

This book is printed on acid-free paper

CONTENTS

LIST OF PLATES

PREFACE TO THE 1985 FRENCH EDITION

It may appear presumptuous to reprint a historical study twenty-seven years after it was first published without making any changes in the text. But I do not believe that what is essential in its conception of the medieval world of universities and scholarship has become outdated. On the contrary, it seems to me that since 1957 the central point of view of this work continues to be confirmed and enriched.

That point of view is first expressed by the word "intellectual," which is of interest in that it shifts attention away from institutions to individuals, away from ideas to social structures, customs, and mentalities, and places the medieval university phenomenon in a longer perspective. Since this book was first published studies on "the intellectual" or "intellectuals" have proved to be more than a passing fashion. As in every pertinent comparatist perspective, if one does not separate the sociological approach, which sheds light on the coherence of types and structures, from the historical approach, which highlights conjunctures, changes, turning points, ruptures, differences, and the insertion of a historical phenomenon into the larger society of an epoch, then the use of the term "intellectual" is justified and useful. In the original edition I did not intend to enter into a theoretical exposé of the idea of the "intellectual," which I had borrowed from the history, sociology, and epistemology of the Western world since the nineteenth century, and I will not open that file now.

Yet it is not by chance that some of the most interesting studies on early "intellectuals" have recently appeared in Gramsci's Italy. Alberto Asor Rosa has provided a general overview;[1] at a Genoese colloquium the idea of "the intellectual" was extended to ancient society;[2] and in a remarkable study Giovanni Tabacco has placed "the medieval intellectual in the interplay of institutions and social forces" at the heart of a volume entirely devoted to intellectuals' relationships with power, part of a history of Italy made available by Gramsci's publisher, Einaudi.[3]

To return to our subject, I am comforted to see Giovanni Santini, in an excellent study devoted to the birth of the University of Modena (the Italian university second only to Bologna at the end of the twelfth century), refer to my 1957 book and state better than I had done: "The birth of 'the intellectual' as a new sociological type presupposes the division of urban labor just as the origin of university institutions presupposes a common cultural space where these new 'cathedrals of knowledge' could rise up, thrive, and confront each other freely".[4]

The division of labor, the town, new institutions, a cultural space common to all western Christian Europe and no longer one contained within the geographical and political divisions of the early Middle Ages – these were the essential traits of the new intellectual landscape of western Christendom at the turn of the twelfth and thirteenth centuries.

The most conclusive aspect of our model of the medieval intellectual is his connection with the town. The scholastic evolution was inscribed within the urban revolution of the tenth to thirteenth centuries. The gulf which separated the monastic school, reserved for future monks, and the town school, in principle open to all, including students who would remain

[1] A. Asor Rosa, "Intellettuali," *Enciclopedia*, VII (Turin: Einaudi, 1979), pp. 801–27.

[2] *Il comportamento dell' intellettuale nella società antica* (Genoa: Istituto di filologia classica e medievale, 1980).

[3] G. Tabacco, "Gli intellettuali del medioevo nel giuoco delle istituzioni e delle preponderanze sociali," *Storia d'Italia, Annali 4*, ed. C. Vivanti, *Intellettuali e potere* (Turin: Einaudi, 1981), pp. 7–46.

[4] G. Santini, *Università e societa nel XII secolo: Pilio da Medicina e lo Studio di Modena* (Modena: STEM Mucchi, 1979), p. 112.

laymen, was fundamental. But I should have discussed at greater length the monastic milieu's attraction to town schools and universities. If from the start the mendicant orders – despite a debate initiated among the Franciscans by St Francis himself concerning poverty and knowledge – flowed into the world of town schools, what is even more significant is the conversion of certain monastic orders (the Premonstratensians and the Cistercians) to university instruction through the establishment of schools for the novices of their orders in university towns beginning in the thirteenth century.

As residents of towns the new intellectuals were professionals. Like merchants, who were "sellers of time," intellectuals, because they were "sellers of words," had to overcome the common belief that knowledge was not to be sold since it was a gift from God. Following the approach of the American medievalist Gaines Post, I have stressed the professional, corporative character of the university masters and students. In addition to the important books by Pearl Kibre, a number of studies have focused on the material, technical, and legal conditions of the university profession.

From this perspective I should have emphasized more the revolutionary character of the university curriculum as a means of recruiting the governing elite. In Western Europe there had been only three means of access to power: birth – the most important; wealth – quite secondary up until the thirteenth century except in ancient Rome; and drawing lots – of limited significance among the citizens of Greek villages in antiquity. In principle the Christian Church granted access to ecclesiastical honors to everyone. In reality, episcopal functions, abbacies, and ecclesiastical dignities were granted in very large part to members of the nobility or the aristocracy. Young nobles and later young members of the bourgeoisie certainly made up the greatest number of students and masters, but the university system also promised real social advancement for a certain number of peasants' sons. It is important, therefore, that studies be devoted to "poor" students. In the typology of poverty, in which great progress has been made thanks to the work of Michel Mollat and his students, univesity poverty represents a special case. An analysis of the reality of its existence and of its role goes beyond the realm of anecdote, and the work of Jean Paquet has been enlightening in this regard. I especially should have pointed out better that such social advancement was accomplished by means of a process which was completely new and revolutionary in Western Europe: *the exam*. The West thus adopted – in a small way – a system which my friend Vadime Elisseeff believes should be studied from a comparatist perspective – that of the Chinese.

The ultimate goal of this professional, social, and institutional evolution was clear: power. Medieval intellectuals did not escape the Gramscian schema which is in truth quite general but operational. In a society which was very tightly controlled ideologically by the Church, and was increasingly governed by a double bureaucracy – secular and ecclesiastical (the greatest "success" in this regard was the pontifical monarchy which, precisely in the thirteenth century, united these two forms), the intellectuals of the Middle Ages were above all "organic" intellectuals, faithful servants of the Church and the state. Universities were increasingly breeding grounds for high functionaries. But since the intellectual function and university "freedom" (despite its limitations) grew around them, a great many of them were more or less "critical" intellectuals, the threshold being that of heresy.

In historically different conjunctures, and with quite original personalities, four great intellectuals of the thirteenth and fourteenth centuries illustrate the diversity of "critical" behavior in the medieval world of higher education: Abelard, Thomas Aquinas, Siger of Brabant, and Wyclif.

I especially should have better studied the formation of university *power* – but unfortunately I had not read the 1951 article by Herbert Grundmann entitled "*Sacerdotium-Regnum-Studium*." And within these three powers – clerical, monarchical, and university – I should also have recognized the trifunctional system which Georges Dumézil has brought to light. In addition to its religious and politico-military functions, knowledge was thus seen as having a function which was, in the beginning, an aspect of its third function, i.e., that of providing affluence, of ensuring a productive economy. It was thus that the intellectual justified himself in theory; he was authorized, like the merchant, to profit from his profession, because of his work, his usefulness, and his creation of consumer goods. The efforts he made as early as the thirteenth century to obtain ecclesiastical power (his insistence on defending his legal status as a *clericus*), and to obtain political influence (available in Paris at the end of the thirteenth century), illustrate the intellectual worker's desire to distinguish himself at all costs, in spite of the fact that medieval intellectuals were themselves tradesmen, as it were, and their very existence depended on the urban workplace. In the time of St Louis the Parisian, Rutebeuf, a marginal intellectual, asserted: "I am not a manual worker."

While attempting to avoid anachronism, I have been led to define the new intellectual work as the joining together, in an urban and no longer monastic environment, of research and teaching. I have thus focused on figures, among all those who out of the masses of teachers and students raised themselves to the heights of scientific and intellectual creation and of great prestige, who appeared at the forefront of the intellectual movement. I was perhaps wrong not to include the popularizers, the compilers, and the encyclopedists, for, having gone through the universities they disseminated the raw material of scholastic research and instruction among the clerks and the learned laymen and through their preaching, among the masses. This is very much a subjective matter. In the Middle Ages, compilation, which is discredited today, was a fundamental exercise of intellectual activity and not simply of the diffusion but also of the invention of ideas. Père Chenu, the great theologian and historian who paved the way for the research which this little book carries on, has little regard for Peter Lombard, the bishop of Paris of Italian origin who died in 1160 and whose book, *Sentences*, which transformed the Bible into a corpus of scholarly knowledge, became the primary theology textbook in universities in the thirteenth century. Yet he appears to me to have been as important an intellectual as was, immediately following him, the Parisian canon Peter Comestor (Peter 'the Devourer'), a devourer of books, who, with his *Historia Scolastica* and other writings, brought together the new intellectual developments of his age into a set of scholarly tools, elementary but fundamental, for future teachers and students.

On the other hand, I am reluctant to rank among the eminent intellectuals of the thirteenth century that Dominican friend of St Louis, Vincent of Beauvais, who in addition to his *Speculum Majus*, the *Mirror of History*, wrote an encyclopedia in which, without any originality of thought, was included all the knowledge of his age, an arsenal for the diffusion of that knowledge among future generations. Nor would I count among them Robert de Sorbon, a Parisian canon, the majority of whose works (especially his sermons) are unpublished, but whose historical importance is in having founded a theological college for twelve poor students, the core of the future Sorbonne, to which he bequeathed his library, one of the largest private collections of the thirteenth century. This Robert de Sorbon, of whom Joinville was jealous because he had to share St Louis's attention with him, and who was constantly reminded by Joinville, a noble, of his peasant origins, was a second-rate "organic" intellectual. But he disseminated well.

I hesitate even more today to draw the line within the intellectual world of the Middle Ages between academics strictly speaking and the "litterateurs" from the thirteenth to fifteenth centuries. I have included Rutebeuf and Jean de Meung, the author of the second part of the *Roman de la Rose*, because as former Parisian students, in their works they echoed the ideological conflicts of the University of Paris in the thirteenth century, and expressed certain important aspects of the "university mentality": a tendency to "reason" (but we must not speak of rationalism); a corporative spirit; anticlericalism – directed above all against the mendicant orders; and a propensity for disputing. And if I had developed my study of intellectuals at the end of the Middle Ages, I would have dealt with that marginal student François Villon. But I regret not having included the great "writers," those instilled with a university training and spirit, a portion of whose works is a product of theology or scientific knowledge. I am thinking above all of Dante, a truly unclassifiable genius, and of Chaucer, in whom scientific curiosity and a creative imagination were equally balanced, even if it is to the latter that he owes his renown.

I especially regret not having focused on these professionals – those no longer at the summit, but rather at the bottom of the intellectual "heap" – who in the twelfth century proclaimed the place of culture in the development of the towns. Besides certain men of the Church, instructors of grammar and rhetoric, lawyers, judges, and especially notaries were among the artisans of the power of towns. Today increasing importance is given, and rightly so, to cultural elements which contributed to the nature and functioning of medieval towns, in addition to economic and strictly juridical and political aspects. The merchant was no longer the only nor perhaps even the primary agent of the urban genesis in the medieval West. All those who through their knowledge of writing, their expertise in law and particularly in Roman law, their teaching of the "liberal" arts and occasionally of the "mechanical" arts, enabled the town to assert itself and, notably in Italy, enabled the commune to become a great social, political, and cultural phenomenon, deserve to be seen as intellectuals of urban growth, one of the principal socio-professional groups to which the medieval town owed its power and its specific character.

Since 1957 valuable studies have appeared which enable us to enrich our knowledge of medieval universities and academics without modifying the framework I proposed. Yet to incorporate them into my work would have led to an almost complete rewriting of the book. In the exhaustive bibliography at the end of this edition the reader will find a list of the most important works to round out my text where necessary.

I will mention three areas in which recent contributions have been particularly significant.

First, that of documentation. Important bibliographies have been published. They notably enable us to become better aware of the university centers which, eclipsed by the "great" universities or located in geographically more or less remote regions, were not commonly known. Prosopographic works, impressive in their volume, have introduced the quantitative into the history of intellectuals in the Middle Ages. The inventory of university

figures having studied at Oxford or Cambridge, of those who
came from Switzerland, Liège, or Scotland, will aid progress in
the history of university geography, and will provide precious
data for social, institutional, and political history. Finally, the
publication of sources or the computerized treatment of certain
sources have started up again following the activity of the end of
the nineteenth century and the beginning of the twentieth, and
will perhaps enable us to modify certain points of view. A recent,
as yet unpublished thesis devoted to the Anglo-German nation
at the University of Paris in the fifteenth century – defended at
the École des Hautes Études en Sciences Sociales by a Japanese
scholar, with the help of André Tuilier, the director of the
Sorbonne's library – promises to alter our image of a University
of Paris in decline at the end of the Middle Ages.

With some exceptions the new bibliography for this edition
does not include references to published documents because
although it is based on lengthy research, this work is not aimed
at scholars. But homage must be paid here to those scholars who
through their labors have provided and continue to provide a
solid foundation upon which to establish the new interpretations
and questions historians are formulating today.

The second area of progress is in the realm of everyday life.
We know much more about where and how masters and
students were housed, how they dressed, what they ate (and
drank), their schedules, their customs, their devotions, their
sexual conduct, their amusements, their deaths and their wills,
and sometimes their funerals and their tombstones. And we also
know more about their working methods and instruments, their
role in the development of techniques of study and their attitudes
toward manuscripts and later printed books. Saenger has shown
how university courses contributed to the medieval reader's
progress from reading out loud to silent reading. An anthropology of medieval intellectuals is being developed.

Finally, the role of universities and academic figures in
politics, a role which became increasingly important after the
thirteenth century, has been made much more apparent. In
France with the succession of the Capetians to the Valois and
with the ravages of the Hundred Years' War (a University of

Paris, collaborating in the assassination of Joan of Arc), in England with barons fighting against kings in the thirteenth century and with dynastic successions in the fourteenth and fifteenth centuries, in the establishment of Czech, Polish and Scots states, in the affairs of the Great Schism and the great councils of Constance and Basel, the university's position as a power – a political power – was firmly established.

My final regret, which is especially great, is in the realm of diachrony. The subject of this study is the emergence and triumph of a new socio-professional figure in the twelfth through thirteenth centuries. I have mentioned the High Middle Ages only as a prehistory of my subject, a barbarous and inarticulate prehistory, and what one no longer dares to call the "Low" Middle Ages, the fourteenth and fifteenth centuries, only as the decline, the betrayal of the earlier model.

I have certainly painted too gloomy a picture, a caricature, in my hasty evocation of the High Middle Ages. In its originality as well as in the long term the Carolingian period did not have its back turned entirely on models comparable, *mutatis mutandis*, to those of the apogee of the Middle Ages, and I have never denied the intellectual reality of a "Carolingian Renaissance," even if its importance has been exaggerated. But I believe that in the Church and the monarchy of the Carolingian period, the nature and function of schools, thinkers, and producers of ideas were very different from what they were with the predominance of urban culture, and that they did not reach beyond restricted aristocratic circles, both ecclesiastical and secular. It would undoubtedly be useful to study in more depth the functioning of urban schools in the tenth and eleventh centuries in the society of that time. In Liège, Reims, and Laon something was taking shape in intellectual activity which prepared for scholasticism, but from the liberal arts to the subjects of the five faculties (arts, medicine, civil and canon law, and theology), from wisdom (*sapientia*) to knowledge (*scientia*, including theological knowledge), there was more discontinuity than continuity. Rather of Verona, Gerbert, and St Anselm shared certain traits with the great intellectuals of the thirteenth century, but the episcopal churches where they reflected and taught were not the

university corporations established in the twelfth century. Looking at the Parisian example, when one goes from Peter Lombard,
from Peter Comestor, from Peter the Chanter to Alexander of
Hales, to William of Auvergne (despite his being the bishop of
Paris), to John of Garland, a new type of "master" emerges.
When one went over to the Left Bank, from the Île de la Cité to
the Latin Quarter, from the school of the cathedral chapter to
the schools of university masters, in just a few dozen years and a
few hundred meters, the landscape changed dramatically.

There was also much that changed, all the while remaining in
the same institutional framework, in the fourteenth and fifteenth
centuries. In this regard my study is completely insufficient and
the work that has been done in this last quarter century will
undoubtedly considerably help to correct it. True, university
instruction in the schools was different from that of the university without buildings of the thirteenth century; true, there was no
longer any dominant doctrine like Aristotelianism (but more
briefly and less completely than was claimed by a neo-Thomist
historiography of scholasticism); true, "reason" took on other
forms at the end of the Middle Ages than it had had at its height.
True, there was a university crisis which was but one aspect of
"the" crisis of the fourteenth and fifteenth centuries and which,
like that crisis, was also before the Black Death of 1348 and
occurred at the turn of the thirteenth and fourteenth centuries,
around 1270–7, undoubtedly accompanied by the doctrinal
condemnations of the bishop Etienne Tempier in Paris. And it is
true, for example, that Gerhard Groot – who was the son of a
rich merchant from Deventer and one of the great adherents of
the *devotio moderna*, new forms of devotion which took hold of the
society at the end of the Middle Ages – after his academic
success at the University of Paris withdrew in 1374 to live among
the Carthusians near Arnhem and expressed violently anti-
university opinions, claiming that knowledge was completely
useless, an instrument of avarice, the ruin of the soul. Only faith
and a simple life could save one's soul.[5] True, there was the

---

[5]   See R.W. Southern, *Western Society and the Church in the Middle Ages* (Harmondsworth:
Penguin Books, 1980), p. 334s.

appearance of a new type of intellectual, the humanist who tended to replace the medieval academic and often asserted himself against the latter. Though this has caused confusion, we are beginning to understand better today, however, that certain academics were also humanists without renouncing the mold from which they had been formed. Gerson and Nicholas of Cusa are perfect examples of this.

What is more, the geographical expansion of the university world modified the university landscape without destroying its framework. In Germanic regions (Vienna in 1383, Erfurt in 1379–92; Heidelberg in 1385; Cologne in 1388; Würzburg in 1402; Leipzig in 1409, etc.), in Bohemia (Prague in 1347), in Poland (Cracow in 1364–1400), not to mention the flourishing of universities in Scotland, Spain, Portugal, France, Italy, etc., new universities were born, based on the Bolognese or Parisian models, the system of faculties or "nations," the distinction between "masters" and "students," etc., although in an often new relationship with towns, states, and organized religion (e.g., the Hussite movement in Prague; the conversion of Lithuanians in Cracow; Averroïsm in Padua, etc.).

If classical scholasticism, and theology in particular, stagnated, and if ecclesiastical control paralyzed universities through its censure of numerous faculties, this was not every-where the case. In the light of certain studies, a Polish one in particular which deals with Cracow, later scholasticism seems to have been more original, more creative, on a higher level than has been claimed. Attendance at universities, far from diminish-ing, grew, even in the large, old universities. The wonderful work done by Jacques Verger and others corrects prevailing concep-tions. The presumed opposition between scholasticism and humanism must be looked at anew. Universities played a more important role in the diffusion of printing than was previously believed.

Most important, the great majority of sources enables us better to study the relationships between universities and socie-ty. In this regard several studies of Oxford and Cambridge are richly informative.

This partial renovation of the university at the end of the Middle Ages (everything would, moreover, be much clearer if the traditional break between the Middle Ages and the Renaissance were abandoned and if we could conceive of an extended Middle Ages continuing until the nineteenth century), and the wealth of information on the social aspects of university life in the fourteenth and fifteenth centuries, are profoundly connected to an essential development of the university milieu. The universities and university masters no longer had a monopoly of intellectual production and higher education. Intellectual circles, like those in the Florence of the Medicis, different colleges, the most illustrious of which was the Collège de France in Paris, nourished and disseminated a predominantly new knowledge under new elitist conditions. Universities granted increasing importance to their *social* role. They trained an increasing number of jurists, doctors, and school masters for states in which new social classes destined for more useful and less brilliant professions required a knowledge better suited to their careers; and for courts which would assure means of support and a reputation for scholars cut off from teaching. The intellectual of the Middle Ages, a product of the town and a university "laborer," destined for the government of a henceforth shattered Christian Europe, disappeared.

Jacques Le Goff

TRANSLATOR'S NOTE

As the reader will note, M. Le Goff makes abundant use of original texts in his essay. Wherever possible I have used the standard English-language translations of those texts, and have cited the appropriate references. When a published translation could not be obtained, I translated directly from the French version.

I wish to thank my friend Robert Williams for his invaluable help with the vocabulary in the section "The Book as Instrument," and David Hopkins for painstakingly editing my translation, and making many valuable contributions to the script. I wish also to thank John Davey for asking me to translate this wonderful "little book."

INTRODUCTION

The *danse macabre* which at the end of the Middle Ages swept away the diverse "estates" of that world – that is, the different social orders – into an emptiness where the sensibility of an age delighted in its decline, often carried along with it kings, nobles, ecclesiastics, the bourgeoisie, the masses, and a clerk who was not always from among the ranks of monks and priests. This clerk was the descendant of a unique lineage in the medieval West: that of the intellectuals. Why has that word been chosen as the title of this little book? It is not the result of an arbitrary choice. Among so many words – savants, scholars, clerk, thinkers (the terminology of the world of thought has always been vague) – "intellectual" designates a milieu with well-defined boundaries: the milieu of school masters. It appeared in the High Middle Ages, developed in the town schools of the twelfth century, and flourished in the universities at the beginning of the thirteenth. It denotes those whose profession it was to think and to share their thoughts. This alliance between personal reflection and its dissemination through instruction characterized the intellectual. Before the present age, that milieu had undoubtedly never been so well-defined, and had never had a better awareness of itself than it did in the Middle Ages. Rather than using the ambiguous term *clericus*, it sought to baptize itself with a name of which Siger of Brabant became the champion in the thirteenth century: *philosophus*, a term I have rejected since for us "philosopher" has a different connotation. The word was borrowed from antiquity. In the age of St Thomas of Aquinas and of Siger, the philosopher par excellence, the Philosopher with a capital "p," was Aristotle. But in the Middle Ages, he was a Christian philosopher. He was the exemplar of that ideal found in the schools of the twelfth to the fifteenth centuries: Christian humanism. But today "humanist" designates another type of scholar, that of the Renaissance of the fifteenth and sixteenth centuries, who in no way identified with the medieval intellectual.

From this present sketch – to which I would have given as a subtitle, if I weren't afraid of being too ambitious and of misusing currently disreputable terms, "An Introduction to a Historical Sociology of the Western Intellectual" – illustrious representatives of the very rich world of medieval thought have been excluded. Nor will mystics secluded in cloisters, or poets and chroniclers uninvolved in the world of schools, immersed in other milieux, appear here, or they will appear only periodically, as points of contrast. Dante, himself, who dominated Western medieval thought, will only cast his immense silhouette here as a shadow puppet. If he attended universities (did he ever really come to Paris, to Rue du Fouarre?), if at the end of the fourteenth century in Italy his works became principal texts for study, if the figure of Siger appeared in his Paradise in verses which appeared strange, he nonetheless followed Virgil beyond the dark forest, on paths other than those cleared or beaten by our intellectuals. More or less influenced by their contact with schools, Rutebeuf, Jean de Meung, Chaucer, and Villon will be evoked here for that reason alone.

It is therefore only one aspect of medieval thought, one type of scholar among others which I will discuss here. I do not deny either the existence or the importance of other groups of thinkers, other spiritual masters. But the intellectual in question seemed so remarkable to me, so significant in the history of Western thought and so well defined sociologically, that his presence and history captured my attention. Moreover, I am quite negligent to put "intellectual" in the singular, since the "intellectuals" were so diverse – as I hope the following pages will show. From Abelard to Ockham, from Albertus Magnus to Jean de Gerson, from Siger of Brabant to Bessarion – so many different, contrasting temperaments, personalities, and interests there were!

A scholar and a professor, a thinker by trade, the intellectual can also be defined by certain psychological traits which could bend the mind, by certain wrinkles in his character which could set and become habits, manias. As a reasoner, the intellectual risked sinking into hair splitting. As a scholar, there was the constant threat of drying up. As a critic, did he not destroy on principle, and denigrate systematically? There is no lack of detractors to turn him into a scapegoat. In the Middle Ages, even if they made fun of fossilized scholastics, critics were not so unjust. They did not impute the destruction of Jerusalem to university scholars nor the disaster at Azincourt to *Sorbonagres*.[1] Beyond reason that age was able to see a passion for the just, beyond knowledge the thirst for truth, and beyond criticism the search for the best. For centuries Dante has responded to the enemies of the intellectual by placing the three greatest intellectual figures of the thirteenth century in a reconciling Paradise: St Thomas, St Bonaventure, and Siger of Brabant.

[1] A slang term used for students and professors at the Sorbonne. – Trans.

1

THE TWELFTH CENTURY

The Birth of the Intellectuals

In the beginning there were the towns. The Western medieval intellectual was born with them. He appeared with the rapid development of the cities and was tied to a commercial and industrial – let us modestly say "artisanal" – function, like the tradesmen who settled in cities where a division of labor prevailed.

In earlier times it was scarcely true that the social classes distinguished by Adalbero of Laon – the one that prays, the clerks; the one that protects, the nobles; and the one that works, the serfs – corresponded to a real specialization among men. The serf, although he cultivated the earth, was also an artisan. The noble, though a soldier, was also a landowner, a judge, and an administrator. And clerks, especially monks, were often simultaneously all of the above. The work of the mind was only one of their activities. It was not an end in itself, but was organized around the rest of their lives, it was directed toward God by the Rule. In the course of their monastic lives they might have temporarily acted as professors, scholars, or writers, but these were fleeting, always secondary aspects of their function. Even those who prefigured the intellectuals of the future were not yet intellectuals themselves. Alcuin was first and foremost a high functionary, Charlemagne's minister of culture. Lupis of Ferrières was primarily an abbot who was interested in books and liked to cite Cicero in his letters.

A man whose profession it was to write or to teach – and usually both at the same time – a man who, professionally, acted as professor and scholar, in short, an intellectual – that man appeared only with the towns.

He truly became identifiable only in the twelfth century. Certainly the medieval town at that time did not sprout forth in Western Europe like a mushroom. Historians have even asserted its complete formation as of the eleventh or tenth century, and each shipment of specialized journals provides evidence of a new urban renaissance, just that much farther back in time.

There have undeniably always been towns in Western Europe, but the "corpses" of Roman towns of the Byzantine Empire enclosed only a handful of inhabitants within their walls, and at their center was a military, administrative, or religious leader. As episcopal cities above all, they contained only a small lay population living among a slightly more numerous clergy, with no other economic life than a small local market serving the daily needs of the inhabitants.

Undoubtedly, in response to the Muslim world, which for its enormous urban clientele – in Damascus, al-Fustat [Old Cairo], Tunis, Baghdad, and Cordoba – required essential materials from the barbarous West – wood, swords, furs, slaves – there developed embryonic towns, *portus*, either autonomous or built on the flanks of the episcopal cities or the military *bourgs* beginning in the tenth, or perhaps even in the ninth century. But this phenomenon became truly significant only in the twelfth century. It then profoundly changed the economic and social structures of Western Europe and began, through the communal movement, to disrupt its political structures, as well.

Another revolution – this time cultural – joined the others. To these births or rebirths there was joined another – an intellectual rebirth. It is the history of its protagonists, the avatars of their successors to the end of what is called the Middle Ages, until another "Renaissance," that this little book aims to sketch.

WAS THERE A CAROLINGIAN RENAISSANCE?

If it is difficult to accept that there was a true, sufficiently well-rounded urban renaissance before the twelfth century, we cannot, while dealing with the realm of civilization, ignore the period – end of the eighth, first half of the ninth century – that has traditionally been called the Carolingian renaissance.

Without going so far as to deny its existence, to speak of a *so-called renaissance*, as certain historians do, we would like to establish its limits.

First, it had none of the quantitative traits of a renaissance which that concept would indicate to us. Although it educated and cultivated the sons of nobles, students at the palace school, and future clerks, in a few of the great monastic or episcopal centers, it practically put an end to what remained of the rudimentary education which the Merovingian monasteries provided to the children from the neighboring countryside. At the time of the great reform of the Benedictine order in 817 inspired by Benedict of Aniane, which stressed the introversion of primitive Benedictine monasticism, the external schools attached to monasteries were closed. It was a renaissance for a close-knit elite – numerically very small – which was intended to give the Carolingian clerical monarchy a small breeding-ground for administrators and politicians. Republican French history textbooks are quite wrong to popularize Charlemagne, who was in any event illiterate, as the protector of the youth of the schools, and as the precursor of Jules Ferry.

Beyond this recruitment of managers for the monarchy and the Church, the intellectual movement of the Carolingian period manifested neither a zeal for propagating new ideas nor disinterest in their use of their newly acquired intellectual tools, or in their general outlook.

The magnificent manuscripts of that time were luxury items. The time spent in copying them in a beautiful script – calligraphy was a sign, even more than was cacography, of an uncultivated age where the demand for books was very

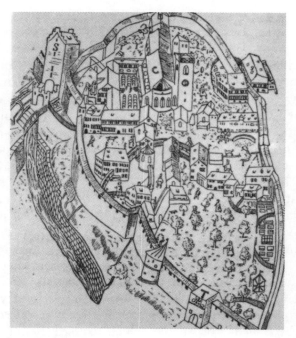

Le monastère de Saint-Gall.

PLATE 1   *The Saint Gall monastery (Bibliothèque nationale)*

small – and in illustrating them splendidly for royalty or for a few great secular or ecclesiastical figures, indicates that books were put into circulation at a very slow pace.

What was more, they were not produced to be read. They were meant to enhance the collections of churches, or of rich individuals. They were an economic, rather than a spiritual possession. Some of the scribes, copying the words of the ancients or of the Fathers of the Church, indeed asserted the superior quality of the works' spiritual content. But owners only took their word for it. And that only added to their material worth. Charlemagne sold a few of his beautiful manuscripts to distribute alms. Books were considered only as precious decorative objects.

The monks who copied them laboriously in the *scriptoria* of the monasteries were only marginally interested in their content – for them what was essential was the effort spent, the time consumed, and the fatigue endured in writing them. It was a work of penance for which they would gain heaven. Moreover, following the taste for a fixed-price evaluation of merits and punishments, which the Church of the High Middle Ages borrowed from barbarous laws, scribes measured the years of purgatory that could be subtracted by the number of pages, lines, and letters written, or, on the contrary, bemoaned the lack of attention which had caused them to skip such and such a letter, thus prolonging their stay in purgatory. They bequeathed to their successors the name of that imp so specialized in teasing them, the demon *Titivillus* of the copyists, whom Anatole France rediscovered.

For these Christians, in whom the barbarian was dozing, knowledge was a treasure. It was to be carefully guarded. A closed culture went hand in hand with a closed economy. Instead of disseminating knowledge, the Carolingian renaissance hoarded it up. Can there be a miserly renaissance?

It was due to a sort of involuntary generosity that the Carolingian period may nevertheless maintain the title of renaissance. Clearly the most original and powerful thinker of that period, John the Scot Erigena, remained without an audience in his time and was only recognized, understood, and made use of in the twelfth century. But then the manuscripts copied in the Carolingian *scriptoria*, the concept of the seven liberal arts borrowed by Alcuin from the fifth-century rhetorician Martianus Capella, his idea of *translatio studii* ["studies in translation"] – picked up by Western Europe, especially by Gaul, from Athens and Rome as the center of civilization – all those gathered treasures were put back into circulation, poured into the cruet of the town schools, absorbed – like the last layer of ancient influence – by the renaissance of the twelfth century.

TWELFTH-CENTURY MODERNITY: THE ANCIENTS AND THE MODERNS

The intellectuals of the twelfth century had the strong feeling that they were doing something new, that they were themselves new men, and is there any renaissance without the feeling of

PLATE 2   *Philosophy and the Liberal Arts, by Herrad of Landsberg*

rebirth? Let us recall those reborn in the sixteenth century, Rabelais, for example.

In their mouths and under their pens, there returned the word to designate the writers of their time: *moderni*, the moderns – this is what they were and knew themselves to be. But they were moderns who had no quarrel with the ancients; on the contrary, they imitated them, were nourished by them, even perched upon their shoulders. "One does not go from the darkness of ignorance to the light of knowledge," wrote Peter of Blois, "without rereading with ever more ardent love the works of the Ancients. Let dogs bark, let pigs grunt! I will remain no less the disciple of the Ancients. All my energy will go toward them, and every morning the dawn will find me studying them."

And here is the basic instruction which was given in Chartres, one of the most famous scholastic centers of the twelfth century, by the master Bernard, as set down in writing by his illustrious student John of Salisbury:

One will more fully perceive and more lucidly explain the charming elegance of the [ancient] authors in proportion to the breadth and thoroughness of his knowledge of various disciplines. The authors by *diacrisis*, which we may translate as "vivid representation" or "graphic imagery," when they would take the crude materials of history, arguments, narratives, and other topics, would so copiously embellish them by the various branches of knowledge, in such charming style, with such pleasing ornament, that their finished masterpiece would seem to image all the arts. Grammar and Poetry are poured without stint over the length and breadth of their works. Across this field, Logic, which contributes plausibility by its proofs, weaves the golden lightning of its reasons; while Rhetoric, where persuasion is in order, supplies the silvery luster of its resplendent eloquence. Following in the path of the foregoing, Mathematics rides [proudly] along on the four-wheel chariot of its Quadrivium, intermingling its fascinating demonstration in manifold variety. Physical philosophy, which explores the secret depths of nature, also brings forth from her [copious] stores numerous lovely ornaments of diverse hue. Of all branches of learning, that which confers the greatest beauty is Ethics, the most excellent part of philosophy, without which the latter would not even deserve its name. Carefully examine the works of Vergil or Lucan, and no matter what your philosophy, you will find therein its seed or seasoning. The fruit of the lecture on the authors is proportionate both to the capacity of the students and to the industrious diligence of the teacher. Bernard of Chartres, the greatest font of literary learning in Gaul in recent times, used to teach grammar in [this] way."[1]

But was that imitation not servility? Later we will see the obstacles created by the introduction of ill-digested, ill-adapted ancient borrowings into Western culture. But in the twelfth century, how new all of that truly was!

If those masters, who were clerks and good Christians, chose to use the writings of Virgil over Ecclesiastes, those of Plato over St Augustine as their textbooks, it was not only because they were convinced that Virgil and Plato were rich in moral

---

[1] John of Salisbury, *The Metalogicon*, translated with an introduction and notes by Daniel D. McGarry (Berkeley: University of California Press, 1955), pp. 66–7 – TRANS.

instruction and that within their bones there was marrow (was there not more in the Scriptures or the writings of the Church Fathers?), it was because they considered the *Aeneid* and *Timaeus* to be primarily *scientific* works written by scholars and intended to be objects of specialized, technical instruction, whereas the Scriptures and the writings of the Church Fathers, which could also be rich in scientific material (was not Genesis a work in the natural sciences and in cosmology?), were only such secondarily. The ancients were *specialists* who found their place better in *specialized* instruction – that of the *liberal arts*, the scholarly disciplines – than did the Church Fathers or the Scriptures, which were to be reserved for the study of theology. The intellectual of the twelfth century was a professional who had his materials – the ancients – and his techniques, the principal one being the imitation of the ancients.

But they were used to advance farther, just as Italian ships used the sea to go to the Orient in search of riches.

Such is the meaning of a famous quote by Bernard of Chartres which had such an effect on the Middle Ages: "We are dwarfs perched on the shoulders of giants. We therefore see more and farther than they, not because we have keener vision or greater height, but because we are lifted up and born aloft on their gigantic stature."[2]

The meaning of the progress of culture – this is what that famous image expressed. In short, it was the meaning of the progress of history. In the High Middle Ages history had stopped, and it was the Church which had become triumphant in Western Europe, the Church that had achieved this. Otto of Freising, taking up the Augustinian concept of the two cities, declared: "From that time on, since not only all men but even emperors, with few exceptions, were Catholics, it seems to me that I have written the history not of two cities but, so to speak, of only one, which I call the Church."[3]

---

[2] Cited in Stephen C. Ferruolo, *The Origins of the University: The Schools of Paris and Their Critics, 1100–1215* (Stanford University Press, 1985), p. 154. – TRANS.

[3] Cited in Le Goff, *Time, Work and Culture in the Middle Ages*, translated by Arthur Goldhammer (University of Chicago Press, 1980), p. 33. – TRANS.

PLATE 3 *Chartres: Windows facing south (13th century). "We are dwarfs perched on the shoulders of giants." (Courtesy Roger Viollet)*

Scholars have spoken of feudal Europe's *will to ignore time* – as well as that of the monks who were integrated into feudal structures. Guizot,[4] having reached the political victory of the bourgeoisie, also believed he had reached the end of history. But the intellectuals of the twelfth century, in those urban surroundings which were slowly rising up, where everything was shifting

---

[4] François-Pierre-Guillaume Guizot (1787–1874), French historian and Statesman. – TRANS.

and changing, put the machine of history back in motion and began by defining their mission in time: *Veritas, filia temporis*, as Bernard of Chartres still said.

THE GRECO-ARAB CONTRIBUTION

The daughter of time, truth is also the daughter of geographic space. Cities are the centers of the traffic of men, full of ideas as well as merchandise, places of exchange, the marketplaces and crossroads of intellectual commerce. In the twelfth century, when Western Europe was still doing scarcely more than exporting raw materials – although textile development was on the rise – rare products, costly objects came from the Orient, from Byzantium, Damascus, Baghdad, and Cordoba. Along with spices and silk, manuscripts brought Greco-Arab culture to the Christian West.

Indeed, Arab culture was initially influential as an intermediary. In the Orient the works of Aristotle, Euclid, Ptolemy, Hippocrates and Galen followed the Christian heretics – Monophysites and Nestorians – and the Jews persecuted in Byzantium, and were relegated to Muslim libraries and schools which by and large welcomed them. They then appeared on a return trip disembarking on the shores of western Christian Europe. The role of the Christian fringe of the Latin states of the Orient was quite secondary. This meeting ground between the West and Islam was above all military, one of armed opposition, the battleground of the Crusades. It was an exchange of blows, not of ideas and books. There were very few written works which filtered through the combat line. Two principal zones of contact accepted Oriental manuscripts: Italy and primarily Spain. In those places neither the temporary installations of the Muslims in Sicily and Calabria nor the waves of the Christian Reconquista ever prevented peaceful exchanges.

Those Christians hunting down Greek and Arab manuscripts ventured as far as Palermo, where the Norman kings of Sicily, then Frederick II, in the midst of their trilingual chancery – where Greek, Latin, and Arabic were spoken – established the first Italian court of renascent Christian Europe,

PLATE 4   *Hippocrates and Galen (Anagni fresco) (Bibliothèque nationale)*

extending as far as Toledo, reconquered from the infidel in 1087, where under the protection of the archbishop Raymund (1125–51) the Christian translators were at work.

THE TRANSLATORS

The translators were the pioneers of this renaissance. Western scholars no longer understood Greek, a fact Abelard deplored, which caused him to beseech the nuns of the Paraclete to fill in that gap, thus going beyond men in the realm of culture. At that time Latin was the language of learning. Original texts in Arabic, Arabic translations of Greek texts, and original Greek texts were thus translated, either by individuals working alone or, more often, by teams of translators. Western Christians sought the assistance of Spanish Christians who had lived under

Muslim rule, the Mozarabs, of Jews, and even of Muslims. Thus all abilities worked together. One of those teams is famous, the one assembled by the illustrious abbot of Cluny, Peter the Venerable, to translate the Koran. Having gone to Spain to inspect the Cluniac monasteries established during the Reconquista, Peter the Venerable was the first to conceive of fighting the Muslims not on the battlefield, but on intellectual ground. In order to refute their doctrine, it first had to be understood. Such an idea, which seems naively obvious to us, was revolutionary in the time of the Crusades.

> Whether one gives the Muslim misconception the shameful name of heresy or the vile name of paganism, we must act against it, that is, we must write. But the Latins, and especially the Moderns, with the ancient culture perishing, as the Jews would say who once admired the polyglot apostles, can speak no other language than that of their native land. Therefore they were able neither to recognize the enormity of that misconception nor stop its progress. Thus my heart is inflamed and a fire has burned in my thoughts. I am indignant to see the Latins ignore the cause of such perdition and to see their ignorance prevent them from being able to resist it; for no one responded, for no one knew how. I thus went in search of specialists in the Arabic language which has enabled this lethal poison to infest more than half the globe. Using pleas and money I persuaded them to translate the history and the doctrine of that unfortunate man and his law which is called the Koran from Arabic into Latin. And to ensure that the translation would be entirely accurate and no errors would hinder our complete understanding, I included a Saracen among the Christian translators. Here are the names of the Christians: Robert of Ketten, Hermann of Dalmatia, Peter of Toledo; the Saracen's name was Mohammed. This team, after thoroughly searching the libraries of that barbarous people, produced a huge book which they published for Latin readers. This work was done during the year I was in Spain, where I had an audience with Alfonso, the victorious emperor of the Spains, in the year of our Lord 1142.

Viewed as an example, Peter the Venerable's undertaking is situated on the margins of the translation movement which

PLATE 5   *Mahomet (drawing by J. Baltrusaitis reproducing the twelfth-century original, taken from* Deux traductions latines du Coran au Moyen Age *by M. T. d'Alverny) (Bibliothèque nationale)*

concerns us here. The Christian translators of Spain were not meeting Islam head-on, but rather were confronting scientific treatises, in both Greek and Arabic. As the abbot of Cluny stressed, he had to pay dearly to avail himself of the services of specialists. They had to be paid handsomely to temporarily abandon their professional work.

How did Western Europe benefit from this first type of researcher, these specialized intellectuals, these translators of the twelfth century? There was James of Venice, Burgundio of Pisa, Moses of Bergamo, Leo Tuscus in Byzantium and in northern Italy, Henry Aristippus of Catania in Sicily, Adelard of Bath, Plato of Tivoli, Hermann of Dalmatia, Robert of Ketten, Hugh of Santalla, Gondisalvi, and Gerard of Cremona in Spain.

They filled in the blanks of Western culture left by the Latin heritage: in philosophy and above all in the sciences. Mathematics with Euclid, astronomy with Ptolemy, medicine with Hippocrates and Galen, physics, logic, and ethics with Aristotle – such was the immense contribution of these laborers. And what was perhaps more important than the content of their work was their method. Their curiosity, their reasoning and all of Aristotle's *Logica Nova* – that of the two *Analytics* (*Prior* and *Posterior*), the *Topics*, and the *Sophistici Elenchi* – was added to the *Logica Vetus*, the Old Logic, known through Boethius, who was also again coming into favor. Such was the shock, the stimulation, the lessons that ancient Hellenism, at the end of its long journey through the Orient and Africa, was communicating to the West.

And we must not omit the purely Arab contribution. Arithmetic with the algebra of al-Khwarizmi – while awaiting the first years of the thirteenth century when Leonardo Pisano would introduce the Arabic numerals, which were actually Hindu but brought from India by the Arabs. Medicine with *Rhazi* – whom the Christians called *Rhazes* – and above all Ibn Sina or Avicenna, whose medical encyclopedia or *Canon* became the inseparable companion of Western doctors. Astronomers, botanists, agronomists, and especially the alchemists who provided the Latins with the feverish research for the elixir. Finally, there was philosophy, which, beginning with Aristotle, created powerful syntheses with al-Farabi and Avicenna. In addition to the works themselves, the Arabs gave the Christians words such as "number," "zero," and "algebra"; at the same time they gave them the vocabulary of commerce; *douane* [custom house], bazaar, *gabelle* [a tax on salt], check, etc.

We can thus understand the exodus to Italy, and especially to Spain, of so many who were thirsting for knowledge, like the Englishman Daniel of Morley who described his intellectual itinerary to the bishop of Norwich:

My passion for knowledge had chased me from England. I stayed for awhile in Paris. There I saw only savages setttled with grave authority on their scholarly seats, with two or three work stands in front of them loaded with enormous tomes reproducing the lessons of Ulpian[5] in golden letters, writing plumes in their hands, with which they gravely painted asterisks and obeli[6] in their books. Their ignorance forced them to remain as still as statues, but they pretended to show their wisdom with such silence. As soon as they opened their mouths I heard only the babbling of babes. Having understood the situation, I sought the means of escaping those risks and of embracing the "arts" which illuminate the Scriptures rather than by greeting them in passing or by avoiding them through shortcuts. Therefore, since at present the instruction of the Arabs, which consists almost entirely of the arts of the *quadrivium* [or sciences], is made available to all in Toledo, I hastened there to attend the lectures of the most learned philosophers in the world. As my friends summoned me back and invited me to return from Spain, I went to England with a precious collection of books. They tell me that in these regions the teaching of the liberal arts was unknown, that Aristotle and Plato were sentenced there to the most profound neglect in favor of Titus and Seius. I felt great anguish at this, and so as not to remain the only Greek scholar among all the Romans, I set off to find a place where I might learn to promote this genre of studies . . .. Let no one be shocked if while dealing with the creation of the world I invoke the teachings not of the Fathers of the Church, but of the pagan philosophers, for, although the latter are not from among the faithful, some of their words, when they evoke sincere faith, should be incorporated into our instruction. We, too, who have been mystically freed from Egypt, the Lord has ordered us to strip the Egyptians of their treasures to enrich the Hebrews with them. Thus, in conformity with the Lord and with his help, let us rob the pagan philosophers of their wisdom and their eloquence, let us rob those infidels to enrich ourselves with their booty in faith.

Daniel of Morley saw only the traditional, decadent, outdated aspect of Paris. There was something else in Paris in the twelfth century.

Spain and Italy knew only a preliminary treatment of Greco-Arab material, that work of translation which was to enable its assimilation by the intellectuals of Western Europe.

---

[5]   Roman jurist, d. AD 228. – TRANS.
[6]   Transfersal signs (— or ÷) with which mistakes were marked.

The centers where Oriental thought was incorporated into Western Christian culture were located elsewhere. The most important were in Chartres and Paris, surrounded by the more traditional ones in Laon, Reims, and Orleans. All were located in that other zone, one of exchange and the perfection of finished products, where the worlds of the North and the South met. Between the Loire and the Rhine, in the very region where great commerce and the bank settled in the markets of Champagne, there developed that culture which was to turn France into the primary heir of Greece and Rome, just as Alcuin had predicted, and as Chrétien of Troyes was proclaiming.

PARIS: BABYLON OR JERUSALEM?

Of all those centers, Paris, favored by the growing prestige of the Capetian monarchy, was the most outstanding. Masters and students rushed either to the Île de la Cité and its cathedral school, or, in growing numbers, to the left bank of the Seine, where they enjoyed greater independence. Around St Julien-le-Pauvre, between the rue de la Boucherie and rue de Garlande; farther east around the school of the Canons Regular of St Victor; to the south, scaling the "Mount" crowned, with its other great school, by the monastery of Ste Geneviève. Alongside the regular masters of the Notre Dame Chapter, the canons of St Victor and Ste Geneviève, the more independent masters, the professors *agrégés* who had received the title of *écolatre*[7] in the name of the bishop, who had the *licentia docendi*, the right to teach, attracted a growing number of pupils and students into their town homes or the cloisters of St Victor or Ste Geneviève which had been made available to them. Paris owed its fame first to the eruption of theological instruction, which was pre-eminent among scholarly disciplines, but it soon owed even more to that branch of philosophy which, taking full advantage of Aristotle's influence and a return to reasoning, brought about the triumph of the rational processes of the mind – the dialectic.

---

[7]   The title of a religious figure directing a cathedral school. – TRANS.

Thus Paris, both concretely and symbolically, was for some the beacon city, the source of all intellectual delights, and for others the den of the devil, where the perversity of minds won over by philosophical depravation joined with the turpitude of a life devoted to gaming, wine, and women. The big city was a den of iniquity; Paris was a modern Babylon. St Bernard implored the masters and students in Paris:

> Flee from the midst of this Babylon, flee and save your souls. All of you, fly to the cities of refuge where you can repent for the past, live in grace in the present, and confidently await the future [that is, in the monasteries]. You will find much more in forests than in books. The woods and the rocks will teach you much more than any master.

And from that other Cistercian, Peter of Celle:

> Oh, Paris, how well you ravish and deceive souls! In you the nets of vice, the traps of evil, the arrows of hell lose the hearts of innocent beings . . . .. Oh what a blessed school [in the cloister], where Christ teaches our hearts with the word of his power, where without study and reading we learn how we should live happily eternally! No book is bought there, a writing master is not hired, there are no convoluted arguments, nor intricate sophisms, but the simple determination of all questions and the simple understanding of all reasons and arguments. There life teaches more than study, simplicity advances more than sophistry.[8]

Thus the holy ignorance party pitted the school of solitude against the school of noise, the school of the cloisters against the school of the town, the school of Christ against that of Aristotle and Hippocrates.

The fundamental conflict between the new clerks of the towns and the monastic milieux (whose restoration in the twelfth century showed extreme tendencies toward primitive monasti-

---

[8] Partial translation in Stephen C. Ferruolo, *The Origins of the University: The Schools of Paris and Their Critics, 1100–1215* (Stanford: Stanford University Press, 1985), pp. 87–8. – TRANS.

PLATE 6 *St Bernard, founder of the abbey (Burgundian school, fifteenth century) (Bibliothèque nationale)*

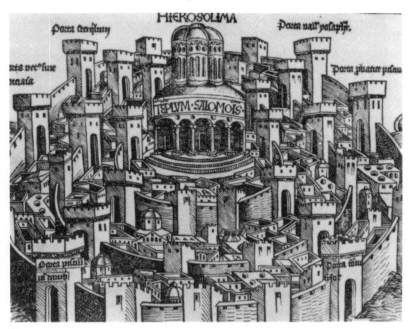

PLATE 7 *Jerusalem*

cism, beyond the development of the western Benedictine movement) burst forth in this exclamation by the Cistercian William
of St Thierry, an intimate friend of St Bernard: "The brothers of
Mont Dieu! They bring the light of the Orient into the darkness
of the West and the religious fervor of ancient Egypt [that is, the
Egypt of St Anthony and early Christian monasticism] to the
coldness of Gaul, that is, the solitary life, the mirror of the life led
in Heaven."

Thus through a curious paradox, just when the intellectuals of
the towns were delving into Greco-Arab culture for intellectual
stimulation and the methods of thinking which would character-
ize the West and create its intellectual strength – a clarity of
thought, a concern with scientific exactness, faith and intelligence supporting each other – monastic spiritualism in the heart
of the West was calling for a return to the mysticism of the
Orient. A crucial moment occurred when the intellectuals of the
towns began to steer the West away from the mirages of another

Orient and another Africa, those of the mystical forest and desert.

But the very withdrawal of the monks paved the way for the development of the new schools. The Council of Reims of 1131 forbade monks to practice medicine outside the confines of the monasteries: Hippocrates was given free reign.

The Parisian clerks did not listen to St Bernard. John of Salisbury wrote to Thomas Becket in 1164:

> I . . . turned my face towards Paris. And there I saw such quantity of food; a people so happy; such respect for the clergy; the splendour and dignity of the whole church; the tasks so diverse of the students of philosophy – saw and marvelled at it, as Jacob marvelled at the ladder whose summit reached to Heaven, which was the path of angles going up and down. The thrill of this happy pilgrimage compelled me to confess: "Truly the Lord is in this place, and I knew it not." It came to my mind how the poet said: "A happy thing is exile in such a place as this."[9]

And the abbot Philip of Harvengt, aware of the enrichment town education could provide, wrote to a young disciple:

> Pushed by the love of knowledge, here you are in Paris and you have found that Jerusalem you so desired. It is the home of David . . . of the wise Solomon. Such a gathering of souls, such a mass of clerks hasten themselves here that they are on the verge of outnumbering the large population of laity. Fortunate city where the sacred scrolls of manuscript are examined with such zeal, where their complicated mysteries are revealed thanks to the gifts of the Holy Spirit, where there are so many eminent professors, where there is such theological learning that one might call it the city of *"belles lettres"*!

THE   GOLIARDS

In this concert of praise for Paris a voice was raised with particular vigor, that of a strange group of intellectuals, the

---

[9]   *The Letters of John of Salisbury*, Volume II, *The Later Letters (1163–1180)*, edited by W. J. Millor, SJ, and C. N. L. Brooke (Oxford: The Clarendon Press, 1979), letter 136, p. 7. – TRANS.

goliards. For them Paris was "Paradise on earth, the rose of the world, the balm of the Universe."

Paradisius mundi Parisius, mundi rosa, balsamum orbis. Who were these goliards? Everything seems to contrive to hide their identities from us. Most are cloaked in anonymity, in legends they eagerly encouraged, those – including much slander and scandalous tales – propagated by their enemies, even those forged by modern scholars and historians, led astray by false resemblances, or blinded by prejudice. Some received the condemnations of the councils and synods and of certain ecclesiastical writers of the twelfth and thirteenth centuries. These goliardic or wandering clerks were called vagabonds, ribalds, jongleurs, and buffoons. They were seen as bohemians, pseudo-students, sometimes viewed with a tender eye – youth must have its day – and sometimes with fear and scorn: agitators, those who held the established order in contempt, were they not dangerous fellows? On the other hand, others saw them as *a sort of urban intelligensia*, a revolutionary milieu, open to all forms of opposition against feudalism. What then was the truth?

If we choose to ignore the origin of the term "goliard" itself, and dispel the fantastic etymologies which derive it from "Goliath," the incarnation of the devil, *the enemy of God*, or from the Latin *gula*, or the French *gueule* [argot term of "mouth"], rendering its disciples "gluttons" and " loudmouths," and recognize the impossibility of identifying a historical Golias, founder of an order of which the goliards would have been members, we still have a few biographical details about certain goliards, collections of poetry placed under their name – both individual and collective efforts such as the *carmina burana* – and contemporary texts which condemn or denigrate them.

INTELLECTUAL VAGABONDAGE

There is no doubt that the goliards created a milieu in which criticism of the established society was eagerly encouraged. Of urban, peasant, or even noble origin, they were primarily wanderers, typical representatives of an age when demographic expansion, the advent of trade, and the development of towns

were destroying feudal structures, bringing together the dis-
placed, the audacious, and the unfortunate, tossing them onto
the roads and the crossroads of the new towns. The goliards were
the fruit of that social mobility characteristic of the twelfth
century. Those escapees from the established structures were a
primary source of scandal to traditionalists. The High Middle
Ages had attempted to put and keep everyone in his place, at his
task, in his order, in his particular condition. The goliards were
escapees. Escapees without means, in the town schools they
formed those groups of poor students who lived by their wits,
became the servants of their more fortunate comrades, survived
by begging, for, as Eberhard the German said: "If Paris is a
paradise for the rich, for the poor it is a swamp eager for prey,"
and he bemoaned the *Parisiana fames*, the hunger of the poor
Parisian students.

To earn a living they sometimes became jongleurs or buffoons,
hence the names they were often given. But we should also
remember that the term *joculator*, or *jongleur*, was at the time the
epithet used for all those who were considered dangerous, whom
one wanted to banish from society. A *joculator* was "a red," a
rebel . . ..

Those poor students who had no fixed home, who had no
prebend, no stipend, thus set out on an intellectual adventure,
following the master who pleased them at the moment, hasten-
ing toward the one currently in fashion, going from city to city to
glean the teachings being offered at the moment. They formed
the body of that scholastic vagabondage that was also so
characteristic of the twelfth century. They contributed to giving
it its adventurous, impulsive, bold appearance. But they did not
form a class. Of different origins, they had different ambitions.
Clearly they chose studying over going to war. But their brothers
went to enlarge the armies; the troops of the Crusades plundered
all along the roads of Europe and Asia, going to pillage
Constantinople. Although everyone criticized them, some, many
perhaps, dreamt of becoming those they criticized. If the poet
Hugh of Orleans, called "the Primate," who successfully taught
in Orleans and Paris and acquired a reputation as a humorless
man, and who inspired the character of the Primasso in the

Decameron, seems always to have led an impecunious life and to have conserved an ever alert mind, then the Archpoet of Cologne lived off Reinald of Dassel, the German prelate who was the arch-chancellor of Frederick Barbarossa whom he lavished with flattery. Serlon of Wilton joined forces with Queen Matilda of England and, having repented, entered Cîteaux.[10] Walter of Lille lived in the court of Henry II Plantagenet, then in that of an archbishop of Reims, and died a canon. They dreamt of a generous patron, a fat prebend, a long and happy life. They seemed to want to become the new beneficiaries of the social order rather than to change it.

IMMORALISM

Nevertheless, the themes of their poetry bitterly attack that same society. It is difficult to deny many of the goliards the revolutionary character that has been found in their poetry. Gaming, wine, love – this is the essential trilogy they praise, which inspired the indignation of the pious souls of their time, but rather inclined modern historians toward indulgence:

> Framed am I of flimsy stuff,
>   Fit for levitation,
> Like a thin leaf which the wind
>   Scatters from its station
>
> Carried am I like a ship
>   Left without a sailor,
> Like a bird that through the air
>   Flies where tempests hale her;
> Chains and fetters hold me not,
>
> For my heart is wounded by
>   Beauty's soft suffusion;
> All the girls I come not nigh,
>   Mine are in illusion.

---

[10] Cîteaux was the original monestery of the Cistercians. – TRANS.

In the second place I own
        To the vice of gaming:
Cold indeed outside I seem,
        Yet my soul is flaming;
But when once the dice-box hath
        Stripped me to my shaming,
Make I songs and verses fit
        For the world's acclaiming.

In the third place, I will speak
        Of the tavern's pleasure;

In the public-house to die
        Is my resolution;
Let wine to my lips be nigh
        At life's dissolution
That will make the angels cry,
        With glad elocution,
"Grant this toper, God on high,
        Grace and absolution!"

These verses may appear harmless and seem only to announce, with lesser genius, Villon. But we must beware: the poem has more piercing characteristics:

Eager far for pleasure more
        Than soul's health, the sooth is,
For this flesh of mine I care,
        Seek not ruth where ruth is.

'Tis most arduous to make
        Nature's self surrender;
Seeing girls, to blush and be
        Purity's defender!
We young men our longings ne'er
        Shall to stern law render,
Or preserve our fancies from
        Bodies smooth and tender.[11]

---

[11] "The Confessions of Golias," no. 5, translation by John Addington Symonds, in *Wine Women and Song*, (London: Chatto and Windus, 1925), p. 67 – TRANS.

Is it rash to recognize here, in this provocative immoralism, in this praise of eroticism – which, among the goliards often went to the point of obscenity – the beginnings of a natural morality, the negation of the teachings of the Church and of traditional morality? The goliard indeed belonged to the large family of libertines who, beyond the freedom of customs and language, sought intellectual freedom.

In the image of the wheel of fortune which often surfaces in the poetry of the wandering clerks, there is something more than a poetic figure; and undoubtedly more than what their contemporaries saw in it, those who represented the image without malice – if not without an ulterior motive – in the cathedrals. However, the wheel of fortune which turns and presides over an eternal return, blind Chance which foils successes, were not in themselves revolutionary themes; they rejected progress, they rejected a direction or meaning to history. They could call for an overturning of society, but it was only insofar as they implied that no interest was taken in the future. Which precisely explains the goliards' taste for these themes – of revolt if not of revolution – these vagabonds who sang of them in their poetry and represented them in their miniatures.

CRITICISM OF SOCIETY

It is significant that goliard poetry – well before their themes became commonplace in secular literature – attacked all the representatives of the established order of the High Middle Ages: the ecclesiastic, the noble, even the peasant.

Regarding the Church, the goliards' favorite targets were those who socially, politically, and ideologically were most closely connected to the structures of society: the pope, the bishop, and the monk.

The goliards' antipontifical and anti-Roman inspiration joined, although it never became a part of, two other contemporary currents of thought, that of the Ghibellines, who primarily attacked the temporal pretentions of the papacy and supported the authority of the German emperors as opposed to the ecclesiastics; and the views of the moralizers who criticized the pontiff and the Roman court for their compromises with the age, for their love of luxury and their taste for money. Granted, there were goliards in the imperial camp, such as the Archpoet of Cologne, and goliard poetry often began as anti-pontifical satires, even when the latter were only bold enough to take up a theme which had become traditional and often lacked sting. But in tone and spirit the goliards distinguished themselves quite clearly from the Ghibellines. In the Roman pontiff and his entourage, they were attacking the head and the guarantors of a social, political, and ideological order, indeed, of every hierarchical social order, for, more than revolutionaries, the goliards were anarchists. From the time the papacy, beginning with Gregorian reform, sought to distance itself from feudal structures and to associate itself more with the new power of money as well as the old power of land, the goliards denounced this new orientation all the while continuing to attack the old tradition.

Gregory VII had declared, "The Lord did not say: 'My name is Custom.'" The goliards accused his successors of making the Lord say: "My name is Money":

Here beginneth the Holy Gospel according to Marks of Silver. At that time the Pope said unto the Romans, "When the Son of Man shall come to the throne of our Majesty, say unto him first, 'Friend, wherefore art thou come?' But if he shall continue knocking without giving you anything, cast him out into outer darkness." And it came to pass that a certain poor clerk came to the court of the Lord Pope and cried out, saying, "Have pity upon me, O doorkeepers of the Pope, for the hand of poverty hath touched me. I am poor and needy, and therefore I beseech you to succor my misfortune and my misery." But when they heard him they were filled with indignation and said, "Friend, thy poverty perish with thee! Get thee behind me, Satan, because thou savorest not what the pieces of money savor. Verily, verily, I say unto thee, thou shalt not enter into the joy of thy Lord till thou hast paid the uttermost farthing."

So the poor man departed and sold his cloak and his tunic and all that he had, and gave unto the cardinals and the doorkeepers and the chamberlains. But they said, "What is this among so many?" and they cast him out, and he went out and wept bitterly and would not be comforted.

Then there came unto the curia a certain rick clerk, who had waxed fat and grown thick, and had committed murder in the insurrection. He gave, first to the doorkeeper, then to the chamberlain, then to the cardinals. But they thought among themselves that they should have received more. Then the Lord Pope, hearing that the cardinals and servants had received many gifts from the clergyman, fell sick nigh unto death; but the rich man sent him a medicine of gold and silver, and straightway he was healed. Then the Lord Pope called unto him the cardinals and the servants and said to them, "Brethren, see to it that no man deceive you with vain words; for, lo! I give you an example that even as I receive, so receive ye also."[12]

Having compromised themselves with the nobility, the clergy then did the same with profiteers. The Church, which had howled with the feudal lords, barked with the merchants. The goliards, voices of that group of intellectuals who in an urban framework sought to promote a lay culture, stigmatized that evolution:

> The Clergy's state has fallen so low
>   The Bride of Christ is put to sale
> From generous sunk to general;
>   What reverence then can laymen show?
> (Sponsa Christi fit mercalis, generosa generalis.)[13]

The weak role of money in the High Middle Ages limited simony. Money's increasing importance made simony a common occurrence.

The satirical bestiary of the goliards, in the spirit of the Roman grotesque, developed a frieze of ecclesiastics metamorphosed into beasts, and highlighted a world of clerical gargoyles

---

[12] Translation in Charles Homer Haskins, *The Renaissance of the Twelfth Century* (Cambridge, MA: Harvard University Press, 1928), p. 185–6. – TRANS.

[13] *The Goliard Poets: Medieval Latin Songs and Satires*, with verse translation by George F. Whicher (Norfolk, CT: New Directions, 1949), p. 133. – TRANS.

on the facade of society. The Pope-lion devoured all, the bishop-calf, a gluttonous pastor, grazed grass before his lambs; his archdeacon was a lynx who uncovered his prey; his dean, a hunting dog who, with the help of officials, hunters for the bishop, stretched the nets and flushed out his prey. Such were the "rules of the game" according to goliard literature.

If the poor curé, considered a victim of the hierarchy and a brother in misery and exploitation, was generally spared by the goliards, the monk was violently taken to task. There was more than just the traditional jokes about monks' bad habits: piggery, laziness, bawdiness. There was a secular tone – close to that of the laity – which denounced monks as competitors who took prebends, penitents, and the faithful away from the poor curés. (This same quarrel, but more finely honed, would be found in the following century in the universities.)

And there was more to the quarrel; there was a rejection of an entire part of Christianity, the part which wanted to cut itself off from the times, which rejected the earth, which embraced solitude, asceticism, poverty, celibacy, and which could even be considered a renunciation of the fruits of the mind. Two types of life were opposed; it was an extreme confrontation between the active life and the contemplative life, paradise prepared on earth and salvation passionately sought beyond this world – this then was the foundation of the antagonism between the monk and the goliard, and was what made the latter the precursor of the Renaissance humanist. The poet of the "Deus pater, adiuva,"[14] who turned a young clerk away from the monastic life, presaged the attacks of a Lorenzo Valla against the *gens cucullata* – the race of cowl-wearers.

A man of the cities, the goliard also voiced his scorn for the rural world and showed only disgust for the gross peasant who incarnated that world and whom he stigmatized in the famous poem, "The Declension of the Peasant":

| Nominative singular | *hic vilanus* | this villein |
| Genitive | *huius rustici* | of this rustic |

[14] A short Latin poem

Dative	*huic tferfero*	to this devil
Accusative	*hunc furem*	this thief
Vocative	*o latro!*	o robber!
Ablative	*ab hoc depredatore*	by this plunderer
Nominative plural	*hi maledicti*	these accursed ones
Genitive	*horum tristium*	of these wretches
Dative	*his mendacibus*	to these liars
Accusative	*hos nequissimos*	these wicked people
Vocative	*o pessimi!*	o evil ones!
Ablative	*ab his infidelibus*	by these infidels[15]

The noble was his final target. The goliard refused him his privilege by birth:

> The noble is he whom virtue has ennobled;
> The degenerate is he whom no virtue has enriched.

As opposed to the old order, the goliard proposed a new order founded on merit:

> The nobility of man is the mind, image of divinity,
> The nobility of man is the illustrious lineage of virtues,
> The nobility of man is the mastery of self,
> The nobility of man is the promotion of the humble,
> The nobility of man are the rights he holds from nature,
> The nobility of man is to fear only turpitude.

The goliard also detested other members of the nobility, the soldier, the military man. For the town intellectual, battles of the mind, and dialectical jousts had become more dignified than feats of weaponry and exploits of war. The Archpoet of Cologne wrote of his repulsion for the military profession (*me terruit labor militaris*), just as Abelard, who was one of the greatest goliard poets, did in texts that were recited and sung on Mount Ste Geneviève the way fashionable songs are hummed today, texts which have unfortunately been lost.

---

[15] Cited in Jacques Le Goff, *Medieval Civilization*, translated by Julia Barrow (Oxford: Basil Blackwell Ltd., 1988), p. 300. – TRANS.

It is perhaps in a realm which is of particular interest to the sociologist that the antagonism between the noble/soldier and the new-style intellectual is best expressed: the relations between the sexes. At the heart of the famous debate between the Clerk and the Knight which inspired so many poems, there is the rivalry of two social groups to win the favor of women. The goliards felt they could not express their superiority over the knights any better than by vaunting the fact that women preferred them over their rivals. "They prefer us, the clerk makes love better than the knight." In this assertion the sociologist must see the clear expression of a struggle between social groups.

In the *Song of Phyllis and Flora,* in which one woman loves a clerk and the other a knight (*miles*), experience makes the heroines conclude, in a judgement which mimics the ritual of courtly love:

> They proceed and all the law's
>   Vigor they pursue,
> Air the court's fixed rules of thumb,
>   Precedents review;
> In accord with what is known,
>   Practices well rooted,
> They declare: to [clerks] is
>   Love much better suited.[16]

In spite of their importance the goliards were relegated to the margins of the intellectual movement of the time. They undoubtedly launched the themes of the future, which were, however, diluted in the course of their long adventure; in the liveliest of ways they represented a milieu eager to be free; they bequeathed to the following century many ideas of natural morality, of a freedom of mores or of thought, of a criticism of the religious society which would be found again among the academics, in the poetry of Rutebeuf, in Jean de Meung's *Roman de la Rose*, and in some of the propositions condemned in Paris in 1277. But they

---

[16] Translation by Edwin H. Zeydel, *Vagabond Verse: Secular Latin Poems of the Middle Ages* (Detroit: Wayne State University Press, 1966), p. 205. – TRANS.

disappeared in the thirteenth century. Persecutions and condemnations targeted them, and their own tendencies toward a purely destructive criticism did not enable them to find their place in a university setting which they sometimes deserted to seek opportunities for an easy living or to indulge in the vagabond's life. The settling of the intellectual movement into organized centers, the universities, ultimately caused this race of wanderers slowly to die out.

ABELARD

Although he was a goliard, Peter Abelard, the glory of the Parisian milieu, meant and contributed much more. He was the first great modern intellectual figure – within the limits of the term "modernity" in the twelfth century. Abelard was the first *professor*.

To begin, Abelard's career, like the man, was remarkable. This Breton from the outskirts of Nantes, born in Le Pallet in 1079, belonged to the petty nobility, for whom life was becoming difficult with the advent of a monetary economy. Abelard gladly abandoned a military career to his brothers and devoted himself to his studies.

If Abelard gave up the weapons of a warrior, it was to engage in another type of battle. Always the fighter, he was to become, in the words of Paul Vignaux, "the knight of dialectics." Always in motion, he went wherever there was a battle to be waged. Always awakening new ideas, he brought enthralling discussions to life wherever he went.

Abelard's intellectual crusade inevitably led him to Paris. There he revealed another trait of his character: the need to destroy idols. His admitted self-confidence – *de me presumens*, he willingly said, which does not mean "to be too presuming," but rather, "being aware of my worth" – led him to attack the most illustrious of the Parisian masters, William of Champeaux. He provoked him, pushed him into a corner, won the students over to his own side. William forced him to leave. But it was too late to stifle that young talent. Abelard became a master. Students followed him to Melun, then to Corbeil, where he ran a school. But his body suddenly failed him, this man who lived only for knowledge; ill, he had to retire for a few years to Brittany.

Having recuperated he went to Paris to look for his old enemy William of Champeaux. There were new jousts; a shaken William modified his doctrine by taking the criticism of his young detractor into account. Abelard, far from being satisfied, intensified his attacks and went so far that he again had to retreat to Melun. But Williams's victory was in fact a defeat. All his students abandoned him. The defeated old master gave up teaching. Abelard triumphantly returned to Paris and settled in the very place where his old adversary had retreated: on Mount Ste Geneviève. The die was cast. Parisian intellectual culture would no longer have the Île de la Cité as its center, but would forever have Mount Ste Geneviève on the left bank: this time a man had established the destiny of a quarter.

But Abelard suffered in not having an adversary at his level. As a logician, he was irritated, moreover, at seeing theologians placed above everyone else. He made an oath: he, too, would be a theologian. He returned to his studies and hurried off to Laon to work with Anselm, the most illustrious theologian of the time. The glory of Anselm did not last long in the presence of the iconoclastic passion of the impetuous antitraditionalist:

I therefore approached the old man who owed his reputation more to his advanced age than to his talent or his culture. All those who approached him to have his advice on a subject about which they were uncertain left him even more uncertain. He was admirable in the eyes of his hearers, but of no account in the sight of questioners. His fluency of words was admirable, but in a sense they were contemptible and devoid of reason. When he kindled a fire he filled his house with smoke, rather than lighted it with a blaze. His tree, in full life, was conspicuous from afar to all beholders, but by those who stood near and diligently examined the same it was found to be barren. To this tree therefore, when I had come that I might gather fruit from it, I understood that it was the fig-tree which the Lord cursed, or that old oak to which Lucan compares Pompey, saying –

There stands the shadow of mighty name,
Like to a tall oak in a fruitful field.[17]

Edified, I did not waste my time at his school.

Abelard was challenged to make good his promise. He took up the gauntlet. He was told that even if he had great knowledge of philosophy, he knew little of theology. Abelard's reply was that the same method could be used for both. His inexperience was pointed out. "I replied that it was not my custom to have recourse to tradition to teach, but rather to the resources of my mind." He then improvised a commentary on the prophesies of Ezekiel which delighted his listeners. People scurried for the notes taken at this lecture to have them copied. A growing audience implored him to continue his commentary. He returned to Paris to do so.

PLATE 8 *Héloïse and Abelard (miniature from* Le Roman de la Rose*) (Musée de Chantilly)*

---

[17] Roger Lloyd, *Peter Abelard: The Orthodox Rebel* (London: Latimer House, 1947), p. 49–50. – TRANS.

HELOISE

Abelard continued his rise to glory – which was abruptly inter-rupted in 1118 by his adventures with Heloise. We know the details of this adventure from Abelard's extraordinary auto-biography *Historia Calamitatum* – "The History of My Troubles" – those premature *Confessions*.

It all began like Cholderlos de Laclos' novel, *Dangerous Liaisons*. Abelard was not a rake. But middle-aged lust attacked this intellectual who, at the age of thirty-nine, knew love only through the books of Ovid and the songs he had composed – in true goliard spirit, but not through experience. He was at the height of his glory and pride. He confessed as much: "I believed there was only myself, the only philosopher in the world." Heloise was a conquest to add to those of his intelligence. And it was at first an affair of the head as much as of the flesh. He learned of the niece of a colleague, the Canon Fulbert; she was seventeen, pretty, and so cultivated that her scholarship was already famous throughout France. She was the woman he was meant to have. He would not have tolerated an idiot, but he was pleased that Heloise was also very pretty. It was a question of taste and prestige. He coolly devised a plan which succeeded beyond his greatest hopes. The canon entrusted the young Heloise to Abelard's care as a pupil, proud to be able to give her such a master. When they discussed his salary Abelard easily convinced the thrifty Fulbert to accept payment in kind: room and board. The devil was keeping watch. There were fireworks between the master and the pupil: first, intellectual exchanges, then, soon after, carnal exchanges. Abelard abandoned his teaching, his work – he was possessed. The affair continued and deepened. A love was born which would never end. It would resist all difficulties, then tragedy.

The first difficulty came when they were caught in the act. Abelard had to leave the home of his deceived host. The lovers met elsewhere. At first hidden, their relationship was soon flaunted. They believed they were above all scandal.

Next, Heloise became pregnant. Abelard took advantage of Fulbert's absence to take his lover, disguised as a nun, to his sister's home in Brittany. There Heloise gave birth to a son whom they called Astralabe (the danger of being the child of a couple of intellectuals . . .).

The third difficulty was the issue of marriage. Abelard, with a heavy heart, would have made amends to Fulbert for his actions by offering to marry Heloise. In his admirable study on the famous couple, Etienne Gilson has shown that Abelard's repugnance was not due to his being a clerk. As an unordained priest he was canonically allowed to have a wife. But Abelard feared that as a married man he would see his academic career hindered, and would become the laughing stock of the scholarly world.

WOMEN AND MARRIAGE IN THE TWELFTH CENTURY

In the twelfth century, there was in fact a very strong antimarriage current. At the same time that women were being liberated, were no longer considered the property of men or as baby-making machines, when the question of whether women had souls was no longer being asked – this was the age of Marian expansion in the West – marriage was the object of disdain, both in noble circles – courtly love, carnal or spiritual, existed only outside marriage; it was embodied in Tristan and Isolde, Lancelot and Guinevere – as well as in scholarly circles, where a complete theory of natural love, later found in the *Roman de la Rose* in the following century, was being developed.

There was a strong female presence, therefore. And Heloise's appearance beside Abelard, while it accompanied the movement supported by the goliards, which demanded the pleasures of the flesh for clerks as well as priests, strongly highlighted an aspect of the new face of the intellectual in the twelfth century. His humanism demanded that he be fully a man. He rejected anything that might appear to be a diminution of his self. He needed a woman by his side to be complete. With the freedom of

their vocabulary, the goliards stressed, with the support of
citations from the two Testaments, that men and women were
endowed with organs whose use should not be made light of.
Disregarding the memory of so many lewd and dubious jokes, we
should think of that climate and psychology, to better grasp the
significance of the tragedy which was to occur, and to better
understand the feelings of Abelard.

Heloise was the first to express her feelings. In a surprising
letter she begs Abelard to reject the notion of marriage. She
evokes the image of the couple of poor intellectuals which they
would form:

> You could not give your attention at the same time to a wife and
> to philosophy. What concord is there between pupils and serving-
> maids, desks and cradles, books or tablets and distaves, styles or
> pens and spindles? Who, either, intent upon sacred or philoso-
> phic meditations can endure the wailing of children, the lullabies
> of the nurses soothing them, the tumultuous mob of the house-
> hold, male as well as female? Who, moreover, will have strength
> to tolerate the foul and incessant squalor of babes? The rich, you
> will say, can, whose palaces or ample abodes contain retreats, of
> which their opulence does not feel the cost nor is it tormented by
> daily worries. But the condition of philosophers is not, I say, as
> that of the rich, nor do those who seek wealth or involve
> themselves in secular cares devote themselves to divine or
> philosophic duties.[18]

Moreover, there were authorities to support this position and
condemn the marriage of the sage. One might cite Theophrastus
or rather St Jerome, who repeated his arguments in *Adversus
Jovinianum*, which was so popular in the twelfth century. And,
joining the Ancient to the Church Father, there was Cicero who,
after rejecting Terentia, refused the sister of his friend Hirtius.

And yet Abelard rejected Heloise's sacrifice. The wedding was
decided, but remained a secret. Fulbert, whom they wished to

[18]   Cited in *The Letters of Abelard and Heloise*, translated from the Latin by C. K. Scott
Moncrieff (New York: Alfred A. Knopf, 1942), pp. 16–17. – TRANS.

appease, was notified, and even attended the nuptial benediction.

But the intentions of the various actors in this drama were not the same. Abelard, with his conscience at peace, wanted to resume his work with Heloise remaining in the shadows. And Fulbert wanted to announce the marriage, make public the satisfaction he had obtained, and undoubtedly weaken the credibility of Abelard, whom he had never pardoned.

Abelard, in distress, conceived of a strategy. Heloise would go into retreat in the convent of Argenteuil, where he had her wear a novice's habit. That would put an end to the stories. In that disguise, Heloise, who had no other will than that of Abelard, waited for the rumors to cease. They had not counted on Fulbert, for he thought he had been tricked. He believed that Abelard had gotten rid of Heloise by having her enter a convent, and that the marriage had been dissolved. One night he led an angry mob to Abelard's house where a crowd gathered, Abelard was mutilated, and the next morning there was a huge scandal.

Abelard went to hide his shame at the royal abbey of Saint-Denis. Remembering what was said above, one can understand the extent of his despair. Could a eunuch still be a man?

We will abandon Heloise here, as she no longer plays a role in the present work. Yet we know how the two lovers, from one cloister to another, continued to exchange the essence of their souls until death did them part.

NEW   BATTLES

His intellectual passion cured Abelard. With his wounds bandaged he once again found his fighting spirit. The ignorant and slovenly monks weighed heavily on him. With his arrogant attitude Abelard weighed equally heavily on the monks, whose solitude was all the more troubled by the many disciples who came to implore the master to resume his teaching again. He wrote his first treatise on theology for them. Its success did not make everyone happy. In 1112 a conventicle[19] in the guise of a council assembled in Soissons to judge it. In a tumultuous atmosphere – to impress the council his enemies had stirred up the mob who threatened to lynch Abelard – in spite of the efforts of the bishop of Chartres who demanded additional information, the book was burned and Abelard was sentenced to end his days in a monastery.

He returned to Saint-Denis, where his quarrels with the monks became increasingly heated. He inflamed them by show-ing that the famous pages by Hilduin on the founder of the abbey were only so much nonsense, and that the first bishop of Paris had nothing to do with Denis of Athens [a.k.a. Dionysius the Areopagite], the Areopagite whom St Paul had converted. The following year he fled the monastery and finally found refuge with the bishop of Troyes. He was given some land, near Nogent-sur-Seine, settled there as a recluse, and built a little oratory to the Trinity. He had forgotten nothing; the condemned book was dedicated to the Trinity.

But his disciples soon discovered his refuge and there was a stampede toward solitude. A scholarly village of tents and huts rose up. The oratory, enlarged and rebuilt out of stone, was dedicated to the Paraclete, which was a provocative innovation. Only Abelard's teachings could make these ersatz country folk forget the satisfactions of the city. They sadly recalled that "in the city students enjoy all the conveniences they need."

Abelard's peace did not last long. Two "new apostles," he said, were organizing a conspiracy against him. They were St Norbert, the founder of the Prémontré, and St Bernard, the reformer of Cîteaux. He was persecuted so harshly that he dreamt of fleeing to the East:

> God knows, I fell into such a state of despair that I thought of quitting the realm of Christendom and going over to the heathen [to go to the Saracens, as is specified in Jean de Meung's translation], there to live a quiet Christian life amongst the

---

[19] Conventicle here has a negative connotation: "an assembly or meeting regarded as having a sinister purpose." – TRANS.

enemies of Christ at the cost of what tribute was asked. I told myself they would receive me more kindly for having no suspicion that I was a Christian on account of the charges against me.[20]

He was spared that extreme solution – the first temptation of the Western intellectual who despairs of the world in which he lives.

He was elected abbot of a Breton monastery, but there were new confrontations. Abelard felt he was living among barbarians. Only Low Breton [the language of Lower Brittany] was spoken there. The monks were unimaginably vulgar. He attempted to refine them. They tried to poison him. He fled from there in 1132.

Abelard appeared once again on Mount Ste Geneviève in 1136. He resumed teaching with more students than ever before. Arnold of Brescia, banished from Italy for fomenting unrest in the towns, took refuge in Paris, joined up with Abelard, and brought his poor disciples, who begged for a living to listen to his teaching. Ever since his book was burned in Soissons, Abelard never ceased to write. It was only in 1140, however, that his enemies again began attacking his works. His ties with the Roman proscript must have been the greatest incitement to their hostility. It is understandable that the alliance of town dialectics and the democratic communal movement would appear significant to his adversaries.

ST BERNARD AND ABELARD

Leading the movement against Abelard was St Bernard. According to the apt expression of Père Chenu, the abbot of Cîteaux "was in another realm of Christendom." That rural man, who remained a medieval and foremost a soldier, was ill-suited to understand the town intelligentsia. He saw only one course of action against the heretic or the infidel: brute force. The champion of the armed Crusade, he did not believe in an

[20] *The Letters of Abelard and Heloise*, translated with an introduction by Betty Radice (Harmondsworth: Penguin, 1974), p. 93–4. – TRANS.

intellectual crusade. When Peter the Venerable asked him to read the translation of the Koran in order to reply to Mohammed in writing, Bernard did not respond. In the solitude of the cloisters he delved into mystical meditation – which he raised to the greatest heights – to find what he needed to return to the world as an administrator of justice. That apostle of the reclusive life was always prepared to fight against innovations he deemed dangerous. During the last years of his life he essentially governed western Christian Europe, dictating his orders to the pope, approving military orders, dreaming of creating a Western cavalry, the militia of Christ; he was a great inquisitor before his time.

A clash with Abelard was inevitable. It was St Bernard's second in command, William of Saint-Thierry, who led the attack. In a letter to St Bernard, William denounced the "new theologian," and encouraged his illustrious friend to pursue him. St Bernard went to Paris, tried to lure Abelard's students away (with the little success so far as we know), and became convinced of the seriousness of the evil Abelard was spreading. A meeting between the two men resolved nothing. One of Abelard's disciples suggested they debate in Sens before an assembly of theologians and bishops. The master undertook once again to uproot Abelard's followers. In secret St Bernard entirely changed the character of the gathering. He transformed the audience into a council, and his adversary into the accused. The night before the opening debate St Bernard assembled the bishops and gave them a complete file showing Abelard as a dangerous heretic. The next day Abelard could only impugn the competence of the assembly and make an appeal to the pope. The bishops communicated a very mitigated condemnation to Rome. Alarmed, St Bernard quickly regrouped. His secretary gave the cardinals, who showed him complete devotion, letters which extracted a condemnation of Abelard out of the pope, and Abelard's books were burned at St Peter's. Abelard learned of this *en route*, and took refuge at Cluny. This time he was broken. Peter the Venerable, who welcomed him with infinite charity, arranged his reconciliation with St Bernard, persuaded Rome to lift his excommunication, and sent him to the monastery of

St-Marcel, in Chalon-sur-Saône, where he died on April 21, 1142. The great abbot of Cluny had sent him written absolution, and in a final gesture of exquisite delicacy, had it sent to Heloise, who was then the abbess of the Paraclete.

Abelard's was a typical existence, while his destiny was extraordinary. From the considerable body of Abelard's works we unfortunately have space to discern only a few remarkable aspects of it here.

THE LOGICIAN

Abelard was foremost a logician, and like all great philosophers he primarily contributed a method. He was the great champion of dialectics. With his *Logica Ingredientibus*, and especially with his *Sic et Non* of 1122, he gave Western thought its first *Discours de la Méthode*. In it he proves with shocking simplicity the necessity of having recourse to reason. The Church Fathers could agree on no issue; where one of them said white, the other said black – *Sic et Non*.

Whence the necessity of a science of language. Words are made to signify – *nominalism* – but they are based on reality. They correspond to the things they signify. The whole effort of logic must consist of making feasible the signifying appropriateness of language to the reality expressed by it. For this demanding mind, language was not the veil of reality, but rather its expression. This professor believed in the ontological value of his instrument, the word.

THE MORALIST

The logician was also a moralist. In his *Ethica seu Scito te ipsum* this Christian, nourished on ancient philosophy, grants introspection as much importance as monastic mystics such as St Bernard or William of Saint-Thierry did. But as de Gandillac has said, "whereas for the Cistercians 'Christian Socratism' was above all a meditation on the impotence of man-the-sinner, self-knowledge appears in the *Ethics* as an analysis of free will through which it is up to us to accept or reject the contempt for God which constitutes sin."

To St Bernard's cries: "Born of sin, of sinners, we give birth to sinners; born of debtors, we give birth to debtors; born corrupt, we give birth to the corrupt; born slaves, we give birth to slaves. We are wounded as soon as we come into this world, while we live in it, and when we leave it; from the soles of our feet to the top of our heads, nothing is healthy in us," Abelard replied that sin is only an omission:

> To sin is to despise the Creator; that is, not to do for Him what we believe we should do for Him, or, not to renounce what we think should be renounced on His behalf. We have defined sin negatively by saying that it means not doing or not renouncing what we ought to do or renounce. Clearly, then, we have shown that sin has no reality. It exists rather in *not being* than in *being*. Similarly, we could define shadows by saying: The absence of light where light usually is.[21]

And he insisted that man has that power to consent, that assent or refusal given to the uprightness which is the center of moral life.

Thus Abelard contributed strongly to questioning the conditions of one of the essential sacraments of the Christian Church: penance. Confronted with a radically evil man, the Church in the barbarous age had made lists of sins and the appropriate punishments, copied from barbarian laws. These *penitentials* attested that, for man of the High Middle Ages, what was essential in penitence was sin, and consequently, punishment. Abelard expressed and strengthened the tendency to inverse that attitude. Henceforth the sinner was most important, that is, his intention, and the primary act of penitence would be contrition. "Sin does not persist," wrote Abelard, "along with this heartfelt contrition which we call true penitence. Sin is contempt

[21] *Abailard's Ethics*, translated with an introduction by J. Ramsay McCallum, M. A. (Merrick, NY: Richwood Publishing Co., 1976), p. 19 – TRANS.

of God or consent to evil; and the love of God which calls forth our grief, allows no vice."[22] The many confessors who appeared at the end of the century had incorporated this reversal in the psychology – if not the theology – of penitence. Thus in the towns and town schools, psychological analysis gained increasing importance and the sacraments were humanized in the fullest sense of the term. What enrichment for the mind of Western man!

THE HUMANIST

Let us stress only one trait of Abelard the theologian. No one ever proclaimed more than he the alliance of reason and faith. In this realm, while awaiting St Thomas, he surpassed the great initiator of new theology, St Anselm, who in the preceding century had set forth his rich formula: faith itself seeking understanding (*fides quarens intellectum*).

In this he satisfied the needs of the scholarly milieux which in theology "demanded human and philosophic reasoning and sought more what could be understood rather than what could be said: of what use, they asked, were words devoid of intelligibility? One cannot believe in what one does not understand, and it is ridiculous to teach others what neither oneself nor one's listeners cannot understand through thought."

During the last months of his life at Cluny, this humanist undertook to write, in great serenity, his *Dialogus inter philosophum, Judaeum et Christianum* ["Dialogue between a Philosopher, a Jew, and a Christian"]. In it he wanted to show that neither original sin nor the Incarnation had caused an absolute break in the history of humanity. He sought to illustrate what the three religions, which for him represented the sum total of human thought, had in common. He aimed to discover the natural laws which, beyond religions, would enable one to recognize the son of God in all men. His humanism culminated in tolerance and,

[22] Ibid., p. 68.

unlike those who were uncompromising, he sought that which connected men, remembering there are "many mansions in the Father's house." If Abelard was the highest expression of the Parisian milieu, we must go to Chartres to discover other traits of the emerging intellectual.

CHARTRES AND THE CHARTRIAN SPIRIT

Chartres was the great center or learning in the twelfth century. The arts of the trivium – grammar, rhetoric, and logic – found their place there, as was seen in the teachings of Bernard of Chartres. But beyond the study of *voces*, words, Chartrian scholars prefered the study of things, *res*, which belonged to the quadrivium: arithmetic, geometry, music, and astronomy.

This orientation determined the "Chartrian spirit," a spirit of curiosity, observation, and investigation which, fed on Greco-Arab knowledge, was to flourish and expand. The thirst for knowledge became so great that the most famous of the popularizers of the century, Honorius of Autun, summed the phenomenon up in a striking phrase: "Man's exile is ignorance; his homeland is knowledge."

This curiosity infuriated the traditionalists. Absalon of St-Victor was shocked by the interest shown in "the conformation of the globe, the nature of the elements, the placement of the stars, the nature of animals, the violence of the wind, the life of plants and roots." William of Saint-Thierry wrote to St Bernard denouncing the existence of people who explained the creation of the first man "not through God, but by nature, spirits, and stars." William of Conches replied: "Ignorant of the forces of nature, they want us to remain bound to their ignorance, to refuse us the right to research, and condemn us to remain fools in believing without intelligence."

Within this movement several great figures from the past were exalted and popularized, figures who, also Christianized, became the symbols of knowledge, the "great mythical ancestors of the scholar."

Solomon was the master of all Oriental and Hebraic knowledge, not only the sage of the Old Testament, but also the great representative of hermetic science under whose name the encyclopedia of magical knowledge was placed; he was the master of secrets, the holder of the mysteries of science.

Alexander was the researcher par excellence. His master, Aristotle, instilled in him a passion for investigation, an exuberant curiosity, the mother of science. An old apocryphal letter was circulated in which he told his master of the marvels of India. They reread the legend of Pliny according to which he had made the philosopher a director of scientific research, placed

PLATE 9   *Alexander in a bathyscape (Musée de Chantilly)*

at the head of a thousand explorers sent to every corner of the world. The thirst for knowledge motivated his voyages, and his conquests. Not content simply to travel over the earth, he wanted to probe the other elements. He was believed to have traveled through the air on a flying carpet. Above all he had a glass barrel made and, going down into the sea in this ancestor of the bathyscaphe, he observed the behavior of fish and studied underwater flora. "Unfortunately," wrote Alexander Neckham, "he did not leave us his observations."

Finally, there was Virgil, the Virgil who announced Christ in the fourth eclogue [of his *Bucolics*] and on whose tomb St Paul prayed, and who assembled into the *Aeneid* the sum total of the knowledge of the ancient world. Bernard of Chartres commented on the first six books of the poem, as if it were a scientific work of the same order as Genesis. Thus the legend was formed which would lead to Dante's admirable character, the one who in the exploration of the underground world was addressed by the author of the *Divine Comedy*: *Tu duca, tu signore e tu maestro.*

The spirit of research did, however, clash with another tendency among the Chartrian intellectuals, that of the rational spirit. On the threshold of the modern age the two fundamental attitudes of the scientific spirit often seemed antagonistic. For the scholars of the twelfth century, experiments only touched on phenomena, on appearances. Science had to turn away from them to grasp reality through reasoning. We will look later at this division which weighed so heavily on medieval science.

CHARTRIAN NATURALISM

The basis of this Chartrian rationalism was a belief in the all-powerfulness of Nature. For the Chartrians, nature was first and foremost a life-giving power, perpetually creative, with inexhaustible resources, *mater generationis*. Thus was established the naturalist optimism of the twelfth century, one of development and expansion.

But Nature was also the cosmos, an organized and rational whole. Nature was the network of the laws whose existence rendered a rational science of the universe both possible and necessary. Another source of optimism was the rationalness of the world, which was believed to be not absurd but incomprehensible, to be not disorder but harmony. The Chartrians' need for order in the universe even led some of them to deny the existence of a primal chaos. This was the position taken by William of Conches and Arnaud of Bonneval, who wrote commentaries on Genesis in these terms: "God, distinguishing the properties of places and names, assigned all things their adequate measures and functions, as if to the limbs of a gigantic body. Even in that distant time [of Creation] there was nothing confused in God, nothing unformed, for the matter of things, as of its creation, was formed into congruent species."

It was in this spirit that the Chartrians made their commentary on Genesis, henceforth explained according to natural laws: physicism vs. symbolism. Chartrians such as Thierry of Chartres who sought to analyze the biblical text "according to physics and to the letter (*secundum physicam et ad litteram*), did this, as did Abelard for his part in his *Expositio in Hexameron*.

For these Christians such beliefs were not without difficulties. There was the problem of the relationship between Nature and God. For the Chartrians God, although He created Nature, respected the laws He had given to it. His all-powerfulness was not contrary to determinism. The miracle acted inside the natural order. "What is important," wrote William of Conches, "is not that God was able to do that, but to examine that, to explain it rationally, to show its goal and usefulness. Certainly God can do everything, but what is important is that he did such and such a thing. Certainly God could make a calf out of the trunk of a tree, as country bumpkins might say, but did He ever do so?"

Thus was pursued a desacralization of nature, a criticism of symbolism, a necessary prolegomenon to all science, which Christianity, as Pierre Duhem has shown, as soon as it began to spread, made possible by ceasing to see nature, the stars, phenomena, as gods – as ancient science had done – but as the creations of a God. The next step stressed the rational character of that creation. Thus, once again, there rose up "against the partisans of a symbolic interpretation of the universe a claim for the existence of an order of autonomous secondary causes under the action of Providence." Certainly, the twelfth century was still replete with symbols, but its intellectuals were already tipping the scales toward a more rational science.

Chartrian Humanism

But the Chartrian spirit was above all humanism. Not only in a secondary sense in that it called upon what was ancient to edify its doctrine; but primarily because it placed man at the heart of its science, its philosophy, and in practice its theology.

For the Chartrians man was the object and the center of creation. Such was the meaning, as Père Chenu has admirably shown, of the *Cur Deus homo* controversy. Opposing the traditional thesis, taken up again by St Gregory, according to which man was an accident of creation, a substitute, a stop-gap, created haphazardly by God to replace the fallen angels after their revolt, the Chartrian school, following St Anselm, proposed the idea that man had always been a part of the Creator's plan and that it was indeed for man that the world had been created.

In a famous text, Honorius of Autun popularized the Chartrian thesis:

> There is no authority other than truth proven by reason; what authority teaches us to believe, reason confirms through its proofs. What the obvious authority of the Scriptures proclaims, discursive reason proves: even if all the angels had stayed in heaven, man with all his posterity would have been created all the same. For this world was created for man, and by world I mean the heavens and the earth and all that is contained in the universe; and it would be absurd to believe that if all the angels had survived the world would not have been created for the one for whom, as we have read, the universe was created.

In passing let us stress that the theologians of the Middle Ages, when they discussed angels – and even their gender – were almost always thinking of man, and that nothing was as important for the future of the mind than these apparently trivial debates.

The Chartrians primarily saw man as a rational being. It was in him that occurred the active union of reason and faith which was one of the fundamental teachings of the intellectuals of the twelfth century. It is from this perspective that I see them being so interested in animals – as the foils of man. The brute/man antithesis was one of the great metaphors of that century. In the Roman bestiary, in that grotesque world which had come from the Orient and which traditional imagery reproduced for its symbolism, the new world of schools saw a reverse humanism – and detached itself from it, moreover, to inspire Gothic sculptors with a new model: man.

We can understand what the Greeks and Arabs contributed to this humanist rationalism. There is no better example in this regard than that of Adelard of Bath, a translator and philosopher, one of the great scholars who journeyed to Spain.

To a traditionalist who in fact proposed discussing animals with him he replied:

It is difficult for me to discuss animals. Indeed, I have learned from my Arab masters to follow reason as a guide, whereas you are content to follow like a captive the chain of a moralizing authority. What else is authority than a chain? Just as stupid animals are led by a chain, and know neither where nor why they are being led, and are content to follow the rope which secures them, thus the majority of you are prisoners of an animal credulity and allow yourselves to be led chained toward dangerous beliefs by the authority of what is written.

And further:

When he wanted to amuse himself, Aristotle would, using dialectical arguments, argue in favor of what was false before his listeners with the aid of his sophistic ability, while the latter defended truth against him. This is because all other arts, if they secure the services of dialectics, can walk sure-footedly, whereas

PLATE 10   *Symbolic animals (Bibliothèque nationale)*

without it they totter and have no stability. Thus in carrying on discussions, the moderns appeal above all to those who are most famous in that art.

Adelard of Bath invites us to go even further. It is not at all certain that the intellectuals of the twelfth century did not themselves create, from the resources of their reason, the essence of what they often camouflaged under the name of the ancients and the Arabs in order better to have their bold ideas accepted by minds used to basing their judgments on authorities – even if they were unpublished. Here is Adelard's confession:

> Our generation has this deep-rooted defect: it refuses to accept anything that seems to come from the moderns. Thus when I have a new idea, if I wish to publish it I attribute it to someone else and I declare: "It is so-and-so who said it, not I." And so that I will be completely believed, I say of all my opinions: "It is so-and-so who invented it, not I." To avoid the disadvantage of people perhaps thinking that I, myself, a poor, ignorant man, derived my ideas from out of my own depths, I make sure they are believed to have come from my Arab studies. If what I've said has displeased backward minds I don't want it to be me who has displeased them. I know what the fate of original thinkers is among the vulgar; thus it is not my case I am presenting, but that of the Arabs.

What was most novel was that this man, endowed with reason, who could therefore study and understand a nature itself rationally ordered by the Creator, was in turn considered by the Chartrians as *nature*, and was thus integrated perfectly into the order of the world.

MAN/MICROCOSM

Thus the old image of *man/microcosm* became invigorated and charged with profound significance. From Bernardus Silvestris to Alan of Lille, there developed the thesis of an analogy between the world and man, between the macrocosm and that universe in miniature that was man. Beyond analyses that bring a smile to our lips, in which the four elements are discovered in the human being, and analogies are pushed to the point of absurdity, that concept was revolutionary. It forced one to consider the whole man, and first of all his body. Adelard of Bath's large scientific encyclopedia dealt at length with human anatomy and physiology. This went hand in hand with and supported progress in medicine and hygiene. Man, whose body had been returned to him, thus welcomed unreservedly that discovery of human love which was one of the great events of the twelfth century, which

PLATE 11   *Man/microcosm, by Hildegard of Bingen (manuscript from the* Liber Divinorum Operum *of Lucca) (Bibliothèque de la Sorbonne)*

Abelard experienced tragically and to which Denis de Rougemont devoted a famous and controversial book. That same man/microcosm was also found at the center of a universe which he reproduced, in harmony with it, suited to guide it, in collusion with the world. Infinite perspectives were open to him, popularized by Honorius of Autun, and perhaps even more by that extraordinary woman, the abbess Hildegard of Bingen, who blended new theories with traditional monastic mysticism in those strange works, *Liber Scivias* and *Liber divinorum operum*. Miniatures, immediately famous, conferred upon these works exceptional significance. Of note is the one which represents man/microcosm in the nude, expressing love for the shape of the body, indicating that the humanism of the intellectuals of the twelfth century did not wait for the next Renaissance to add that dimension in which the aesthetic taste for forms joined with a love of true proportions.

The final word of this humanism was clearly that man, who was nature, who could understand nature through reason, could also transform it through his actions.

THE FACTORY AND "HOMO FABER"

The intellectual of the twelfth century, placed at the center of the urban workplace, saw a universe in the image of that place, a vast factory humming with the noise of workers. The stoic metaphor of the world/factory was taken up again in a more dynamic environment with more useful significance. In his *Liber de aedificio Dei*, Gerhoch of Reichersberg speaks of "this great factory, this great workshop, the universe" (*illa magna totius mundi fabrica et quaedam universalis officina*).

Man asserted himself in that workplace as an artisan who transformed and created – a rediscovery of *homo faber*, who with God and nature cooperated in all creation. "All work," said William of Conches, "is the work of the creator, the work of nature, or of man-the-artisan imitating nature."

And the image of human society was also being transformed. Perceived in this dynamic perspective which gave meaning to the economic and social structures of the age, society was to integrate all human workers. In that rehabilitation of work, those scorned in the past were integrated into the human polis, the image of the divine polis. In his *Policraticus*, John of Salisbury returned rural workers to society: "those who always cleave to the soil, busied about their plough-lands or vineyards, or pastures, or flower-gardens"; then the artisans: "the many species of cloth-making, and the mechanic arts, which work in wood, iron, bronze, and the different metals."[23] In this perspective the old scholarly framework of the seven liberal arts burst apart. The new instruction had to make place not only for the new disciplines – dialectics, physics, ethics – but also for the scientific and artisanal techniques which were an essential part of man's activity. In the program of studies outlined in his *Didascalion*, Hugh of St-Victor confirmed this new concept. Honorius of Autun developed it in his famous phrase: "Man's exile is ignorance; his homeland is knowledge." Indeed he added, "one reaches it through the liberal arts, which are so many way stations." The first station was grammar, the second, rhetoric, the third, dialectics, the fourth, arithmetic, the fifth, music, the sixth, geometry, and the seventh, astronomy. There was nothing new in that. But the road was not complete. The eighth was physics, "in which Hippocrates teaches the pilgrims the virtues and the nature of grasses, trees, minerals, and animals." The ninth was mechanics, "where the pilgrims learn the working of metals, wood, marble, painting, sculpture, and all the manual arts. It is there that Nemrod raised his tower and Solomon built the Temple. It was there that Noah built his ark, taught the art of fortifications and the working of various cloths." The eleventh was economics. "It is the door of the homeland of man. In it one regulates states and dignities, one distinguishes functions and orders. In it one teaches men who hasten toward their homeland how, in the order of their merits, to join the hierarchy of the angels." Thus the humanist odyssey of the intellectuals in the twelfth century ended with politics.

INTELLECTUAL   FIGURES

While discussing the intellectuals, even those in Chartres, we should point out their different personalities and temperaments. Bernard was foremost a professor concerned with giving his students basic instruction and methods of thinking through solid

---

[23]   John of Salisbury, *Policraticus: The Statesman's Book*, abridged and edited, with an introduction by Murray F. Markland (Frederick Ungar, New York, 1979), p. 91. – TRANS.

grammatical training. Bernardus Silvestris and William of Conches were primarily *scientists* – good representatives in this regard of the most original tendency of the Chartrian spirit. In their time they were balanced by the literary spirit, so seductive for so many. As Abelard said to Heloise: "More concerned with teaching than with eloquence, I seek the clarity of the exposition, not the ordering of eloquence; a literal meaning, not rhetorical ornamentation." This was a principle followed by translators who revolted against beautifying infidels. "I have neither pruned nor altered in a notable way the material you needed to construct your magnificent edifice," wrote Robert of Chester to Peter the Venerable, "and if so, only to make them understood . . . and I have not tried to cover a vile and despicable material with gold." John of Salisbury, however, was a humanist more in the sense which has become familiar to us, showing pleasant refinement and an ease of expression. Although he was a Chartrian he was a literary man. Above all he sought to maintain a healthy balance: "Just as eloquence unenlightened by reason is reckless and blind, knowledge which does not know how to use words is weak and crippled. Men would become beasts if they were deprived of the eloquence with which they have been endowed."

Gilbert de la Porrée was a thinker, perhaps the most profound metaphysicist of the century. His misfortunes – he was also the victim of the traditionalists and of St Bernard – did not prevent him from inspiring many disciples (among the Porretians were Alan of Lille and Nicholas of Amiens) or from inciting the fervor of the people as well as that of the clerics in his diocese of Poitiers.

CHARTRIAN INFLUENCE

Above all Chartres, formed pioneers. In Paris, following the storms raised by Abelard, moderate thinkers attempted to incorporate all that could be borrowed from the innovators into the traditional teachings of the Church without causing a scandal. This was primarily the task of the bishop Peter Lombard and Peter Comestor – whose reputation as a devourer

PLATE 12   *Peter Lombard*

PLATE 13   *Peter Comestor*

of books was well-founded. The former's *Sentences* and the latter's *Historia Scholastica* – systematic treatments of philosophical truths and historical facts contained in the Bible – were to be the fundamental texts for university instruction in the thirteenth century. Through them the majority of the prudent would nevertheless benefit from the discoveries of the small number of the bold.

THE INTELLECTUAL WORKER AND THE URBAN WORKPLACE

It was only within an urban framework that this type of intellectual could develop. His adversaries, his enemies knew this well, those who encompassed into a same curse the cities and this new genre of intellectuals. Stephen of Tournai, the abbot of Ste Geneviève at the end of the century, was alarmed at the inroads of *disputatio* into theology: "Contrary to the sacred canons there is public disputation as to the incomprehensible deity; concerning the incarnation of the Word . . .. The indivisible Trinity is cut up and wrangled over in the trivia, so that now there are as many errors as doctors, as many scandals as classrooms, as many blasphemies as squares."[24] "Sellers of words (*venditores verborum*)" he also said about the Parisian masters.

He thus echoed the thoughts of the abbot of Deutz, Rupert, who at the beginning of the century, having learned that he was being mocked in the town schools, had valiantly come out of his cloister and faced his enemies in the city. There, on every corner of every street he immediately saw debates, and foresaw the diffusion of evil. He reminded his listeners that all builders of towns were impious, and instead of camping on this temporary abode, the earth, they were settling there and inviting others to join them. Going through the entire Bible, he derived a grandiose anti-urban fresco. After the first city built by Cain, after Jericho which was brought crumbling down by the holy trumpets of Joshua, he listed Enoch, Babylon, Ashur, Nineveh, Babel . . . God, he said, did not like cities or city-dwellers. And the cities of his time, teeming with vain disputes between

[24] Lynn Thorndike, *University Records and Life in the Middle Ages* (New York: Columbia University Press, 1944), p. 23. – TRANS.

masters and students, were only the resurrection of Sodom and Gommorah.

Comparable to other city-dwellers, the town intellectual of the twelfth century indeed felt like an artisan, a professional man. His function was to study and teach the *liberal arts*. But what was an *art*? It was not a science, but a technique. *Ars* was "τεχνη", the specialty of the professor as of the carpenter or the welder. In the next century, following in the footsteps of Hugh of St-Victor, St Thomas experienced all the consequences of that position. An *art* was any rational and just activity of the mind applied to the manufacturing of instruments, both material and intellectual; it was an intelligent technique for "doing" or "making." *Ars est recta ratio factibilium.* Thus the intellectual was an artisan; as Hugh of St-Victor wrote in the *Didascalicon* "among all the sciences, [the liberal arts] are called arts because they do not imply just knowledge, but also a production which unfolds immediately from reason, like the function of construction (grammar), syllogisms (dialectics), discourse (rhetoric), numbers (arithmetic), measurement (geometry), melodies (music), calculations of the course of the stars (astronomy)."

The day when Abelard, reduced to misery, admitted he was incapable of working the land and that he was ashamed of begging, he returned to teaching (*scolarum regimen*): "Reverting to the art which I knew, instead of the labour of my hands, I was driven to the office of my tongue."[25]

RESEARCH AND TEACHING

A professional man, the intellectual was conscious of the profession he had undertaken. He recognized the necessary link between knowledge and teaching. He no longer believed that knowledge should be hoarded, but was persuaded that it should be put into circulation. Schools were workshops out of which ideas, like merchandise, were exported. In the urban workplace the professor rubbed elbows in a same productive capacity with

[25]   Moncrieff, *The Letters of Abelard and Heloise*, p. 35.

the artisan and the merchant. Abelard reminded Heloise that it was the Philistines who kept their knowledge to themselves and prevented both themselves and others from benefitting from it:

> Let us return to Isaac and dig with him wells of living water, even if the Philistines obstruct us; even if they use violence, let us carry on with our well-digging, so that to us too it may be said: "Drink water from your own cisterns and your own wells" (*Proverbs* V 15). And let us dig until our wells overflow with water in our courtyards, so that our knowledge of the Scriptures is not only sufficient for ourselves but we can teach others and show them how to drink.[26]

This was the generosity of the intellectual. He knew he was the first to benefit from it. "If I have been able to write this book," wrote Hermann of Dalmatia to a friend, "it is because I have had to sustain the insidious assaults of adversaries in the public schools."

TOOLS

In that great factory, the universe, the intellectual, in his place and with his own abilities, had to cooperate in the creative work which was unfolding. Moreover, he had no other tools than his mind and his books, which were his particular tools. How far things had progressed from the oral teachings of the High Middle Ages! Gerald of Wales declared:

> Today illiterate clerks are like nobles unfit for war. They remain dumbfounded at the sight of a child's book as before a sudden theatrical spectacle, for they are unaware that these are the instruments of clerks, whereas the blacksmith knows that fishing lines are the instruments of fishermen and the fisherman knows that the anvil and the hammer are instruments of the blacksmith; neither one can exercise the art of the other, but they can both name the other's instruments, despite their ignorance of the instruments' use or technique.

[26] Radice, *The Letters of Abelard and Heloise*, p. 267.

It remained for those artisans of the mind, drawn into the urban development of the twelfth century, to become organized in the midst of the great corporative movement which was crowned by the communal movement. Those corporations or "colleges" of masters and students became, in the strict sense of the word, the *universities*. They were the great work of the thirteenth century.

PLATE 14   *Albert the Great, by Justus of Ghent*

2

THE THIRTEENTH CENTURY:

Maturity and its Problems

The thirteenth century was the age of the universities because it was the age of corporations. In any town where there was a profession bringing together a large number of members, they organized to defend their interests, and to establish a profitable monopoly. This was the institutional phase of medieval urban development which solidified acquired political freedoms into communes, and economic advantages into guilds. The word freedom here is ambiguous: was it independence or privilege? The same ambiguity will be seen again in the university corporation. Corporative organization then fixed what it had consolidated. As the consequence of and authorized by progress, that organization lost its verve and succumbed to decadence. Such was the case for the universities in the thirteenth century, in accord with the trends of the age. Demographic expansion was at its height, but was slowing down; and the population of western Christian Europe would soon stabilize. The great wave of land clearing which had provided the land needed to feed this human surplus, slowed down and stopped. A surge of construction raised a series of new churches for this larger Christian population, churches showing a new spirit, but the era of the great Gothic cathedrals ended in the previous century. The university's evolution followed the same curve: after the thirteenth century, Bologna, Paris, and Oxford were never to have as many masters and students, and the university method, scholasticism, would raise no more brilliant monuments than the *summae* of Albert the Great, Alexander of Hales, Roger Bacon, St Bonaventure, and St Thomas of Aquinas.

The intellectual who established his place in the town nonetheless proved incapable, faced with the choices available to him, of choosing solutions for the future. In a series of crises which one might attribute to growth, and which were the warnings of maturity, he was unable to opt for rejuvenation, and settled into social structures and intellectual habits in which he became bogged down.

The origins of university corporations are often as obscure as those of other professional bodies. They were organized slowly, by violent, successive conquests, by chance incidents which were only so many unexpected opportunities. Statutes often belatedly sanctioned these conquests. And we are not always sure that the statutes we possess were the first. There is nothing surprising in all this. In the towns where they were formed, the universities, through the number and quality of their members, manifested a strength which worried the other powers. It was only by fighting, sometimes against ecclesiastical powers, sometimes against lay powers, that they won their autonomy.

AGAINST ECCLESIASTICAL POWERS

University academics were clerks. The bishop of the area claimed them as subjects. Teaching was an ecclesiastical function. The bishop, head of the schools, had for a long time delegated his powers in the matter to one of his officers who was generally called an *écolâtre* [see note on p. 22] (*scolasticus*) in the twelfth century, and who was soon after called a chancellor. The chancellor was reluctant to relinquish any control. When that control was no longer absolute, when abbeys acquired a strong scholastic position, they created other adversaries within the university corporation. Indeed, culture was a matter of faith; the bishop insisted on retaining control of it.

In 1213 in Paris the chancellor practically lost the privilege of conferring the *license*, that is, the authorization to teach. This right was bestowed upon the university masters. In 1219, when members of the mendicant orders were admitted into the university, the chancellor attempted to oppose that innovation. In the attempt he lost his last remaining prerogatives. In 1301 he even ceased to be the official head of the schools. At the time of the great strike of 1229–31 the university was withdrawn from the jurisdiction of the bishop.

At Oxford, the bishop of Lincoln, at a distance of 120 miles from the university, officially presided over it through his intermediary, his chancellor, whereas the abbot of the monastery of Oseney and the prior of St Frideswide held only honorific positions. But soon the chancellor was absorbed by the university, elected by it, and became its officer instead of working for the bishop.

In Bologna the situation was more complex. For a long time the Church had been uninterested in the teaching of law, which was considered to be a secular activity. It was only in 1219 that the archdeacon of Bologna, who seems to have filled the function of chancellor and was sometimes designated by that name, became the leader of the university. But his authority was in fact outside of the university. He was restricted to presiding over promotions, and to absolving offenses against its members.

AGAINST LAY POWERS

University corporations also had to fight against lay powers and primarily against royal authority. Rulers sought to lay their hands on corporations which brought wealth and prestige to their kingdoms, and which formed breeding-grounds out of which their officers and functionaries would come. Rulers wanted to impose an authority upon those inhabitants of their states, i.e., the academics of the towns in their kingdoms, an authority which, with the progress of monarchical centralization in the thirteenth century, was being increasingly felt by their subjects.

In Paris the autonomy of the university was definitively achieved after the bloody events of 1229, which set students against the royal police. In one confrontation several students were killed by the royal soldiers. Most of the university went on strike and moved to Orleans. For two years there were almost no courses given in Paris. It was only in 1231 that St Louis and Blanche of Castile solemnly recognized the university's independence and renewed and extended the privileges that Philip Augustus had granted it in 1200.

In Oxford, thanks to the excommunicated John Lackland's eclipse of power, the university obtained its first liberties in 1214. A series of conflicts in 1232, 1238, and 1240 between academics and the king ended with the capitulation of Henry III, who was intimidated by the support part of the university had given to Simon of Montfort.

But there were also struggles against communal power. The bourgeoisie of the commune was irritated in seeing the university population escape from their jurisdiction; they were concerned about the racket, the plundering, the crimes of certain students, and ill tolerated the fact that masters and students limited their economic power by having rents taxed, by imposing a ceiling on the price of commodities, and by having justice respected in commercial transactions.

In Paris in 1229 the royal police had to brutally intervene following brawls between students and the townsmen. In Oxford in 1214 the university took the first steps toward independence following the arbitrary hanging of two students in 1209 by townsmen exasperated after the murder of a woman. And in Bologna the conflict between the university and the townsmen was all the more violent since the commune until 1278 had governed the city almost exclusively, under the distant rule of the emperor who, in 1158, in the person of Frederick Barbarossa, had accorded privileges to masters and students. The commune had imposed perpetual residence on professors, had turned them into functionaries, and had intervened in the conferring of degrees. The increasing authority of the archdeacon limited the commune's meddling in university affairs. A series of conflicts followed by strikes and the departure of academics seeking refuge in Vicenza, Arezzo, Padua, and Siena brought the commune to terms. The last confrontation took place in 1321.

The university no longer had to put up with communal interventions.

How did university corporations emerge victorious from those battles? First, through their cohesion and determination, and also by threatening to use and by effectively using those fearful weapons, the strike and secession. Civil and ecclesiastical powers found too many advantages in the presence of academics – who represented an important economic clientele, a unique breeding-ground for counselors and functionaries, a bright source of prestige – to resist these tactics of defense.

THE SUPPORT AND CONTROL OF THE PAPACY

But more important, the academics found an all-powerful ally in the papacy.

In 1194 in Paris, Celestine III granted the corporation its first privileges, and it was primarily Innocent III and Gregory IX who assured its autonomy. In 1215 the papal legate Cardinal Robert de Courçon, gave the university its first official statutes. In 1231 Gregory IX, who accused the bishop of Paris of

PLATE 15   *The pope and the emperor granting privileges at the University of Bologne (Bibliothèque de la Sorbonne)*

negligence and forced the king of France and his mother to give in, granted new statutes to the university through the famous bull *Parens scientiarum*, which has been called the university's "Magna Carta." As of 1229 the pontiff had written to the bishop:

> Whereas a man learned in theology is like the morning sun which shines through the fog and must illuminate his homeland with the splendor of the saints and settle discord, you were not content simply to neglect this duty, but, according to the assertions of trustworthy souls, it is due to your machinations that the river of the teaching of "*belles-lettres*" which, after the grace of the Holy Spirit, waters and fertilizes the paradise of the universal Church, has left its bed, that is, the city of Paris, where it was vigorously flowing up to now. Subsequently, divided in several places, it has been reduced to nothing, like a river which has left its bed and is divided into several creeks, dries up.

In Oxford it was likewise a legate of Innocent III, Cardinal Nicholas of Tusculum who granted the beginnings of the university's independence. Against Henry III, Innocent IV placed it "under the protection of St Peter and the Pope," and ordered the bishops of London and Salisbury to protect it against royal schemes.

PLATE 16   *Proceedings instituted by the pope against a bishop (miniature from Gratian's* Decretum*)*

In Bologna Honorius III placed the archdeacon at the head of the university who defended it against the commune. The university was definitively emancipated when in 1278 the city of Bologna recognized the pope as its ruler.

This pontifical support was a fact of primary importance. The Holy See undoubtedly recognized the importance and value of intellectual activity, but its interventions were not disinterested. If it rescued academics from secular jurisdictions, it was to place them under those of the Church: thus, to obtain that decisive support, intellectuals found themselves forced to choose the path of ecclesiastical adherence, against the strong current which was pushing them toward secularity. If the pope released the academics from the local control of the Church – not entirely, however, for we will see the importance, throughout the century, of episcopal condemnations in the intellectual realm – it was to subject them to the Holy See, to integrate them into its politics, to impose its control and its ends upon them.

Thus the intellectuals became subject, like the new religious orders, to the apostolic see which showed them favor in order to domesticate them. We know how in the course of the thirteenth century pontifical protection turned the mendicant orders away from their original principles and goals. We especially know of the reservations and the painful retreat of St Francis of Assisi in the face of his order's deviation, an order which was henceforth engaged in temporal intrigues, in the forcible repression of heretics, in Roman politics. It was also the end of independence for the intellectuals, the end of the disinterested spirit of study and teaching. Without going as far as the extreme case of the University of Toulouse, established in 1229 upon the express request of the popes to fight against the Albeginsian heresy, all universities henceforth endured that unrequested legacy. They certainly gained independence with regard to local forces which were often relatively more tyrannical, they witnessed the widening, in accordance with the growing dimensions of all of Western Christianity, of their horizons and their influence, and they were subject to a power which on many occasions proved to be quite open-minded. But they paid dearly for these gains. Western intellectuals had, to a certain extent, but most definitely, become agents of the pope.

INTERNAL CONTRADICTIONS OF THE UNIVERSITY CORPORATION

Let us now examine what was unique to the university corporation, that which explained its fundamental ambiguity in society, and made it prone to structural crises.

It was essentially an ecclesiastical corporation. Even if all its members had not received orders, even if it counted among its ranks an increasing number of pure laymen, academics were essentially all clerks, answerable to ecclesiastical authorities, and primarily to Rome. Born of a movement heading toward secularity, they were of the Church, even when they sought to leave it institutionally.

A corporation whose goal was a *local* monopoly and which benefitted largely from national or local developments (the University of Paris was inseparable from the growth of Capetian power, Oxford was linked to the strengthening of the English monarchy, and Bologna benefitted from the vitality of Italian communes), it was, in a unique way, *international*. This is seen in its members – masters and students came from many different countries – in the subject of its activity – knowledge which knew no geographical boundaries – in its horizons, which were sanctioned by the *licentia ubique docendi*, the right to teach anywhere, a statute from which the graduates of the largest universities benefitted. Unlike other corporations, it did not have a monopoly on the local market. Its territory was the western Christian world.

Thus the university corporation already went beyond the urban framework in which it was born. What is more, it was led to confront townsmen – sometimes violently, sometimes on an economic level, sometimes on jurisdictional and political levels.

The corporation thus seemed destined to straddle social classes and groups. It seemed destined, with regard to all groups, for a series of betrayals. For the Church, for the State, for the City, it might be a Trojan Horse. It was unclassifiable.

"The city of Paris," wrote the Dominican Thomas of Ireland at the end of the century, is, like Athens, divided into three parts: the first, that of the merchants, artisans, and the populace, which is called the main city; next, that of the noblemen, in which the king's court and the cathedral church are found, which is called the Île de la Cité; the third, that of the students and the colleges, which is called the University.

ORGANIZATION OF THE UNIVERSITY CORPORATION

The Parisian university corporation can be considered as a typical example. In the course of the thirteenth century it defined both its administrative and its professional organization. It was made up of four faculties (*arts*, *law*, or rather *canon law* – Pope Honorius III forbade the teaching of civil law in 1219 – *medicine*, and *theology*) which formed as many corporations or colleges inside the university. The so-called "superior" faculties – law, medicine, and theology – were directed by titular masters or "regents" with a "dean" at their head. The arts faculty, with by far the most members, was founded on the system of "nations." Masters and students were grouped according to a distribution corresponding quite loosely to their place of

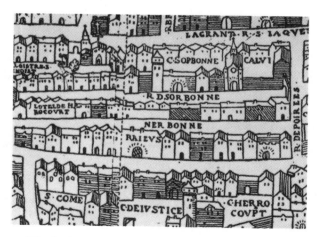

PLATE 17   *The Sorbonne and its surroundings (map by Basel) (Bibliothèque de la Sorbonne)*

birth. Paris had four nations: France, Picardy, Normandy, and England. At the head of each nation was a "proctor" who was elected by the regents. The four proctors assisted the "rector," the head of the faculty of arts.

There were, however, aspects of university life shared by the four faculties. These nevertheless remained somewhat dormant since the faculties had few problems to settle in common. There was no property or buildings belonging to the university corporation as a whole, with the exception of the Pré-aux-clercs playing field outside the walls. The university, like the faculties and the nations, met in churches or in monasteries where it was welcomed as a guest: in the church of St-Julien-le-Pauvre, at the Dominican or the Franciscan convent, in the chapter-house of the Bernardines or the Cistercians, more often in the Mathurines' refectory, where a general assembly of the university composed of regent and non-regent masters often met.

In the course of the fourteenth century there finally emerged a head of the university: the rector of the faculty of arts. We shall later return to the evolution which caused that faculty to become the leader of the university. It owed its preeminence to its greater number of members, to its guiding spirit, and even more to its financial role. The rector of the arts faculty, who controlled the university's finances, presided over the general assembly. At the end of the century he was the recognized head of the corporation. He definitively earned that position in the course of struggles between secular masters and the regular clergy; we shall return to this later. However, his authority was always limited in time. Although he could be reelected, he held his office for only one trimester.

Often with considerable variations, we find this same organization at other universities. At Oxford there was more than one reactor. The "chancellor" was the head of the university, chosen quickly, moreover, as we have seen, by his colleagues. As of 1274 the system of "nations" had disappeared in Oxford. Undoubtedly its eminently regional recruitment explains this. Henceforth northerners or *Boreales* – including the Scots – and southerners or *Australes* – including the Welsh and Irish – no longer formed distinct bodies within the corporation.

The first peculiarity was found at Bologna: the professors were not formally a part of the university. The university corporation included only students. The masters formed the "college of doctors." Actually, Bologna included several universities. Each faculty formed a separate college. But the preponderance of the two jurist colleges – teaching civil and canon law – was almost total. That preponderance was reinforced throughout the century by the fact that there was an almost complete fusion of the two branches. A single rector was most often at the head of the university. As in Paris he came out of the system of "nations," which was very lively and very complex at Bologna. The nations were grouped into two federations, the Cismontanes and the Ultramontanes. Each contained a variable number of nations – as many as sixteen for the Ultramontanes, represented by the councillors (*consiliarii*) who played an important role along with the rector.

The university corporation derived its power from three essential privileges: jurisdictional autonomy – within the framework of the Church, with certain local restrictions, and the power to appeal to the pope; the right to strike and to secede; and the monopoly of conferring university degrees.

THE ORGANIZATION OF STUDIES

The university statutes also determined the organization of studies. They defined the number of years of study, the program of courses, and the nature of exams.

Information concerning the age of students and the number of years they studied is unfortunately imprecise and often contradictory. It has varied depending upon time and place, and scattered allusions lead us to believe that practice was often quite far from theory.

First, at what age did one enter the university, and with what intellectual baggage? Surely at a very young age, but it is here that the problem is raised: were grammar schools indeed a part of the university system, was the teaching of writing, for example, provided before a student entered the university, or, as Istvan Hajnal claims, was it one of the university's essential functions? One fact is certain: the Middle Ages did not make a clear distinction in the levels of instruction. Medieval universities were not uniquely establishments of higher learning. What we consider as primary or secondary instruction was offered in part at the universities, and was controlled by them. The system of "colleges" – of which we shall speak later – confused the issue even more by dispensing instruction to its members beginning at the age of eight.

In general one can say that at the universities basic instruction – that of the "arts" – lasted six years and was offered between the ages of fourteen and twenty; this is what the Paris statutes of Robert de Courçon stipulated. He delineated two stages in university education: the baccalaureate after around two years, and the doctorate at the end of one's studies. Medicine and law were then undoubtedly taught between the ages of twenty and twenty-five years old. The first statutes of the faculty of medicine in Paris stipulated six years of studies to obtain the license or doctorate in medicine – once the master-of-arts had been obtained. Finally, theology was a long-term proposition. Robert de Courçon's statutes ordered eight years of study and a minimum age of thirty-five to obtain the doctorate. In fact, it seems that the theologian had to study for fifteen or sixteen years: he was a mere auditor for the first six years, and then had to complete the following training: four years of Bible explication, and two years of studying and commenting on Peter Lombard's *Sentences*.

PROGRAMS OF STUDY

Since instruction consisted essentially of the explication of texts, statutes also mentioned the works to be included in the program of university studies. Here, again, the authors varied depending upon time and place. In the faculty of arts, logic and dialectics were most important, at least in Paris where almost all of Aristotle was studied, whereas in Bologna only excerpts from

that author were explicated. In Bologna rhetoric was emphasized with Cicero's *De Inventions* and *Ad Herennium*, as were the
mathematical and astronomical sciences, notably Euclid and
Ptolemy. Among the law students, Gratian's *Decretum* was the
basic textbook. The Bolognese added Gregory IX's *Decretals*, as
well as the *Clementines* and the *Extravagants*. In civil law, commentaries were based on the three-part Pandects – the *Digestum
Vetus*, the *Infortiatum*, and the *Digestum Novum* – on the Code, and
on a collection of treatises known as the *Volumen* or the *Volumen
Parvum* which included the *Institutiones* and the *Authentica*, that is,
the Latin translation of Justinian's Novels. The University of
Bologna also added the Lombard *Liber Feudorum*. The faculty of
medicine relied upon the *Ars medecinae*, a collection of texts
assembled in the eleventh century by Constantinus Africanus
which included the works of Hippocrates and Galen, to which
were later added the great Arab *summae*: Avicenna's *Canon*,
Averroës' *Colliget* or *Correctorium*, and Rhazes' *Almansor*. In
addition to the Bible, theologians added Peter Lombard's *Sentences* and Peter Comestor's *Historia Scholastica* as their primary
texts.

EXAMS

Finally, there were regulations for exams and for the earning of
degrees. Again, each university had its own practices, and
modified them over time. Here are two typical scholarly curric-
ula: that of the Bolognese jurist and the Parisian "artist." The
new Bolognese doctor earned his degree in two stages: the exam
in the strict sense (the *examen* or *examen privatum*) and the public
examination (the *conventus*, *conventus publicus*, or *doctoratus*), which
was rather a ceremony of investiture.

Some time before the private examination, the candidate was
presented by the *consiliarius* of his nation to the rector, to whom
he swore that he had complied with all the statutory conditions,
and that he was not seeking to corrupt his examiners. In the
week preceding the exam, one of the masters presented him to
the archdeacon, thus guaranteeing the student's ability to

undergo the trial. The morning of the exam, after attending a Mass of the Holy Ghost, the candidate appeared before the college of doctors, one of whom assigned him two passages to comment on. He went home to prepare that commentary, which he presented the same evening in a public place (most often in the cathedral), before a jury of doctors, and in the presence of the archdeacon, who could take no active part in the exam. After the required exposition he responded to the questions of the doctors, who then exited and voted. The decision being taken by a majority vote, the archdeacon then announced the results.

Having passed the exam, the candidate became a licentiate, but was not given the title of doctor and could not truly teach authoritatively until after the public exam. Driven in pomp to the cathedral on the day of the public examination, the licentiate delivered a speech and read a thesis on a point of law which he then defended against the students who attacked him, thus assuming for the first time the role of master in a university disputation. The archdeacon then solemnly conferred upon him the license to teach, and he was given the *insignia* of his function: a chair, an open book, a golden ring, and the magisterial *biretta* or beret.

A preliminary degree was given to the young Parisian "artist." Though we cannot confirm this with certainty, it is probable that it was after an initial exam, the *determinatio*, that the student became a "bachelor." The *determinatio* was preceded by two preliminary tests. First of all, the candidate had to engage in a debate with a master during a *responsiones* which took place in the December before the Lent during which the *determinatio* would take place. If the candidate successfully completed the test, he was admitted to the *Examen determinantium* or *Baccalariandorum*, where he had to prove that he had satisfied the statutory requirements, and show, through his responses to the questions of a jury of masters, that he was familiar with the authors included in his program. That step taken, there then came the *determinatio*. During Lent he gave a series of lectures in which he had to show his ability to pursue a university career.

The second stage was the examination in the strict sense which led to the license and to the doctorate. This, again, involved several phases. The most important one consisted of a series of commentaries and responses to questions given before a jury of four masters presided over by the chancellor or the vice chancellor. A few days later the successful candiate solemnly received the license from the hands of the chancellor during a ceremony in which he had to give a lecture (*collatio*) which was only a formality. It was around six months later that he actually became a doctor during the *inceptio* which corresponded to the Bolognese *conventus*. The day before he took part in a solemn disputation called his "vespers." The day of the *inceptio* he gave his inaugural lecture in the presence of the faculty and received the *insignia* of his status.

Finally, the university statutes included a whole series of stipulations which, just like other guilds, defined the moral and religious climate of the university corporation.

THE MORAL AND RELIGIOUS CLIMATE

The statutes stipulated – while they also limited – collective festivities and amusements. Exams were in fact accompanied by gifts, celebrations, and banquets – with the expenses met by the new "inceptor" – which confirmed the spiritual communion of the group and the admission of the new student into its fold. Like the drinking parties, the *potaciones* of the first guilds, these celebrations were a ritual in which the corporation became aware of its profound solidarity. The university tribes revealed themselves in these games where each country sometimes contributed a traditional flavor: masked balls in Italy, bull fights in Spain, etc.

There were also initiation rituals, not set down in statutes, which welcomed the new student – the rookie, the freshman, whom our texts call a *bejaunus* – upon his arrival at the university. We know of them through a curious later period document, the *Manuale Scolarium*, written at the end of the fifteenth century, in which we can discern the distant origins of these student customs. The initiation of the novice is described as a ceremony of "purging" intended to strip the adolescent of his primitive rusticity, of his bestiality. Other students made fun of his smelling like a wild animal, of his bewildered gaze, of his long ears, his fang-like teeth. "Horns" and other assumed growths were removed from him. He was washed, his teeth cleaned. In a parody of confession he ultimately admitted to extraordinary vices. Thus the future intellectual abandoned his original condition, which strongly resembled the images of the peasant, the country bumpkin found in the satirical literature of the time. From bestiality to humanity, from rusticity to urbanity, these ceremonies, in which, degraded and practically emptied of its original content, the old primitive essence appeared, recall that the intellectual had been extracted from a rural environment, from an agrarian civilization, from a rude, uncivilized life on the land. The anthropologist would have something to say in a psychoanalysis of the clerks.

UNIVERSITY PIETY

Statutes also determined the pious works, the charitable acts which the university corporation was to accomplish. They required its members to participate in certain religious offices, in certain processions, and in the maintaining of certain devotions.

Certainly of greatest importance was piety with regard to the patron saints, primarily to St Nicholas, the patron of students, to Saints Cosmas and Damian, the patrons of doctors, and to many others. Showing singular persistence, one finds in university imagery a corporative tendency to intimately blend the sacred world with the profane world of professions. Images evoked Jesus among doctors, represented saints equipped with the accoutrements of masters, dressing them in magisterial robes.

University piety was an integral part of the great currents of spirituality. In the statutes of the fourteenth-century Parisian college *Ave Maria*, we note the participation of masters and students in the fully-developed eucharistic devotion, and in the procession of *Corpus Christi*.

Beginning in the thirteenth century, one finds this tendency toward spirituality in the religion of intellectuals in the professional trades which the urban world was defining. Professional morality became one of the privileged sectors of religion. Confessors' manuals, eager to adapt to the specific activities of social groups, regulated confession and penance according to professional categories, classified and defined the sins of peasants, merchants, artisans, judges, etc. They paid special attention to the sins of intellectuals, of academics.

But the religion of the clerks was not content to follow the currents of ecclesiastical devotions. It sometimes sought to direct them, or to define a sector among them which would suit the clerks. In this regard it would be enlightening to study Marian piety among intellectuals. It was very strong in the universities. In the university milieux from the beginning of the thirteenth century poems and prayers were circulated which were dedicated especially to the Virgin, of which the *Stella Maris* collection, by the Parisian master John of Garland, is the most famous. There is nothing surprising in a piety which contributed a feminine presence to a milieu which, despite the heritage of the goliards, was essentially one occupied exclusively by men – unmarried men. But the Marian piety of the intellectuals had unique characteristics. It always remained impregnated with theology, and its discussions on the Immaculate Conception were quite heated. If Duns Scotus was its empassioned

PLATE 18 *Rutebeuf praying to the Virgin (Bibliothèque nationale)*

champion, it encountered the dogmatic opposition of St Thomas Aquinas, who, moreover, followed in this the position of St Bernard, the great devotee of the Virgin in the preceding century. It seems, above all, that the intellectuals were concerned with conserving intellectual resonances for the Marian cult. They appeared hopeful of avoiding its fall into a too affective piety and wanted to maintain in it a balance between the aspirations of the mind and the élan of the heart. In the preface to the *Stella Maris*, John of Garland naively betrays that tendency:

> I have assembled the miracles of the Virgin as excerpted from tales I have found in the collections of Ste Geneviève in Paris, and I have put them in verse form for my Paris students in order to provide them with a living example . . .. The material cause of this book are the miracles of the glorious Virgin. But in it I have included facts which concern physics, astronomy, and theology . . .. The final cause indeed resides in a permanent faith in Christ. Therefore, it implies theology and even physics and astronomy.

This much is clear: the academics wanted that *Star of the sea* [*Stella Maris*] also to be the light of knowledge.

THE   TOOLS   OF   THE   TRADE

As a tradesman, the member of the university corporation in the thirteenth century was equipped with a complete set of tools. A writer, a reader, a professor, he surrounded himself with the instruments required by his activities. We read in the Dictionary of the Parisian master John of Garland:

> Here are the instruments needed by clerks: books, a desk, an evening lamp with tallow and candle holder, a lantern, and an inkwell with ink, a pen, a plumb bob and ruler for ruling lines, a table, and a ferule, a chair, a blackboard, a pumice stone along with an erasing knife, and chalk. The desk (*pulpitum*) is called a lectern (*letrum*); we must note that the desk is equipped with a

notched device which enables it to be raised to the height at which one reads, for one places the book upon the lectern. The iron instrument with which parchment makers prepare the parchment is called a scraping knife (*plana*).

Other instruments have been found, ones which, even if they were not used by all clerks, were among the tools of his adjuncts, the copyists, for example: notably a scrap of parchment and a place marker enabling one to find the spot in the text where one had left off copying.

As a specialist, the intellectual weighed himself down with a whole set of baggage which distanced him from the clerk of the High Middle Ages, whose essentially oral education required only very minimal paraphernalia for writing a very few manuscripts, the technique of which was based primarily on aesthetic concerns.

Although oral exercises continued to be essential in university education, the book became the basis of instruction. One understands, in seeing the paraphernalia with which the intellectual henceforth surrounded himself, that St Francis of Assisi, the apostle of privation, was, for many reasons, hostile to that activity for which material equipment became so necessary and increasingly overwhelming.

THE BOOK AS INSTRUMENT

The university book was very different from the book of the High Middle Ages. It was connected to a completely new technical, social, and economic context. It was the expression of another civilization. Writing itself changed and was adapting to the new conditions, as Henri Pirenne points out:

> Cursive writing responded to a civilization in which writing was indispensable to the life of the collectivity as well as to that of individuals; the miniscule (from the Carolingian period) was a writing style appropriate to the learned class in whose circle instruction was confined and perpetuated. It is highly significant

to note that cursive writing reappeared beside it in the first half of the thirteenth century, that is, precisely at the time when social progress and the development of the lay economy and culture once again universalized the need for writing.

The wonderful work of Père Destrez[1] has shown the significance of the revolution which was occurring in the thirteenth century in the technique of the book, a revolution whose theater was the university workshop.

Not only were the authors on the syllabus to be read by the masters and students, but the professors' lectures had to be preserved. The students took notes (*relationes*) and we possess a certain number of them. What was more, these lectures had to be published rapidly so that they could be consulted at the time of exams, and they also had to be produced in a certain number of copies. The basis of this work was the *pecia*. Let us read Père Destrez's description of it:

> A first official copy of the work which was to be put into circulation was written in unbound signatures of four folios. Each one of these signatures, made out of sheepskin folded into quarters, bore the name of the piece, i.e., *pecia*. Thanks to these separate signatures, which the copyists borrowed one after the other, and when they were collated were called the *exemplar*, the same amount of time which had previously been necessary for a single copyist to make only one complete copy, became sufficient, when dealing with a work which contained some sixty signatures, for around forty scribes to make that many copies of a correct text under the control of the university and which then became in a certain sense the official text.

This publication of the official text of lectures was of primary importance in the universities. In 1264 the statutes of the University of Padua declared: "without copies there would be no university."

The increasing use of books by academics brought with it a whole series of consequences. Progress achieved in the making of

---

[1] *La Pecia dans les manuscrits universitaires du XIII et du XIVs* (Paris: 1935).

parchment enabled the production of thinner, more supple, and less yellow sheets than those of earlier manuscripts. In Italy, where the technique was more advanced, pages were very thin and brilliantly white.

The format of the book changed. Earlier it was clearly in folio size. "It was a dimension which could only suit manuscripts written in abbeys and which were to remain there." Henceforth the book was often consulted, carried from one place to another. It became smaller, more manageable.

The more rapidly written Gothic miniscule replaced the older writing style. It varied according to the university centers; there was the Parisian, the English, the Bolognese. It also corresponded to a technical progress: the abandonment of the reed for the quill pen, generally from a goose, which allowed for "greater ease and rapidity in writing."

The ornamentation of books became less common: illuminated initials and miniatures were done in series. Although law texts often remained luxurious, since jurists in general belonged to a richer class, the books of philosphers and theologians, who were most often poor, only rarely contained miniatures. Often the copyist left a blank place for initials and miniatures so that a buyer of modest means could purchase the manuscript as it was, while a richer client could commission illuminations for the empty spaces.

In addition to these significant details, there was a growing abundance of abbreviations – it was necessary to produce quickly – and there was progress in page-numbering, in rubrication, in the listing of contents, the occasional presence of a list of abbreviations, and recourse, whenever possible, to an alphabetical ordering in the presentation. Everything was put in motion to facilitate rapid consultation. The development of the intellectual profession produced an era of the handbook – of a "handy" book which could be held in one's hand – a dazzling testimony to the acceleration of the speed of circulation of the written culture and its diffusion. An initial revolution was accomplished: the book was no longer a luxury item, it had become a tool. It was a birth, more than a rebirth, which anticipated the printing press.

As a tool, the book had become an industrial product and a commercial object. In the shadow of the universities there developed a whole population of copyists – they were often poor students who thus earned their livelihood – and of book sellers (*stationarii*). Indispensable to the university workplace, they were admitted there as workers in their own right. They were able to benefit from the same privileges as academics, and came under the jurisdiction of the university. They swelled the ranks of the corporation, enlarged it with an entire margin of auxiliary artisans. The intellectual industry had its adjunct and secondary industries. Some of those producers and merchants were already great figures. Next to "artisans whose activity was reduced to the resale of a few used works," others "enlarged it to the role of an international publisher."

THE SCHOLASTIC METHOD

Along with his instruments the intellectual technician had his methodology: scholasticism. Illustrious scholars, at the forefront of whom is Grabmann, have described its formation and its history. Père Chenu, in his *Introduction à l'étude de Saint Thomas d'Aquin*, has given a lucid exposé of scholasticism. We shall attempt to sketch an outline of it here, and to assess the significance of this scholasticism which was a victim of secular condemnation and which is so difficult to approach without some background, so off-putting are its technical aspects. The words of Père Chenu can serve as a clue: "Thinking is a *profession* whose laws are minutely fixed."

VOCABULARY

First, there were laws of language. If the famous controversies between the realists and the nominalists obsessed medieval thinking, it is because the intellectuals of that age endowed words with a rightful power and were concerned with defining their content. They wanted to know what relationships existed between the word, the concept, and the being. As opposed to this, there is nothing more contrary than the concern with verbalism, of which scholasticism has been accused and into which it did sometimes fall in the thirteenth century and often afterwards. The thinkers and teachers of the Middle Ages wanted to know what they were talking about. The basis of scholasticism was grammar. The scholastics were the heirs of Bernard of Chartres and Abelard.

DIALECTICS

Next there were laws of demonstration. The second stage of scholasticism was dialectics, an ensemble of processes which turned the object of knowledge into a problem, which exposed it, defended it against attackers, untangled it and convinced the listener or the reader. The danger here was empty reasoning – no longer verbalism, but verbiage. It was necessary to give dialectics a content not only of words, but of efficient thought. University figures were the descendants of John of Salisbury who said: "Dialectic . . . if studied alone, remains lifeless and sterile, nor does it stimulate the soul to bear fruits of Philosophy unless it conceives elsewhere."[2]

AUTHORITY

Scholasticism was fed on texts. It was a method based on authorities, and it rested upon the dual contribution of earlier civilizations: Christianity and ancient thought enriched, as we have seen, by the Arab detour. It was the fruit of a moment, of a renaissance. It digested the past of Western civilization. The Bible, the Fathers of the Church, Plato, Aristotle, the Arabs, all were the givens of knowledge, the material for the work at hand. The danger here was in mindless repetition, in servile imitation.

---

[2] Cited in *The Medieval University 1200–1400* by Lowrie J. Daly, SJ, with an introduction by Pearl Kibre (New York: Sheed and Ward, 1961), p. 222 – TRANS.

From the intellectuals of the twelfth century the scholastics inherited a sharp sense of the necessary and inescapable progress of history and thought. With those materials they undertook their work. To older foundations they added new floors, original buildings. They were of the lineage of Bernard of Chartres, perched on the shoulders of the ancients in order to see farther. "Never," said Gilbert of Tournai, "will we find the truth if we are satisfied with what has already been found . . .. Those who wrote before us are not our lords, but our guides. Truth is open to all; it has not yet been possessed in its entirety." An admirable élan of intellectual optimism, as opposed to the sad "All has been said, and we have arrived too late . . ."

REASON: THEOLOGY AS "SCIENCE"

Scholasticism joined the laws of reason to those of imitation, and the arguments of science to the dictates of authority. What was more, and this was decisive progress in the century, theology appealed to reason, it became a "science." The scholastics developed the implicit invitation of the Scriptures which incited the believer to explain and justify his faith: "Be ready always to give an answer to every man that asketh you a reason of the hope that is in you" (I Peter 3:15). They responded to the call of St Paul for whom faith was the "evidence of things not seen" (*argumentum non apparentium* [Hebrews 11:1]). After William of Auvergne, an initiator in this realm, and until St Thomas, who was to turn theological science into the most definitive exposé, the scholastics resorted to theological reason, "reason en-lightened by faith" (*ratio fide illustrata*). The famous formula of St Anselm, *Fides quaerens intellectum*, "faith itself seeking understand-ing," was made clear when St Thomas set forth his principle, "grace does not make nature disappear, but completes it" (*gratia non tollit naturam sed perficit*).

There was nothing less obscurantist than a scholasticism in which reason led to understanding, whose sparks of illumination were perfected in light.

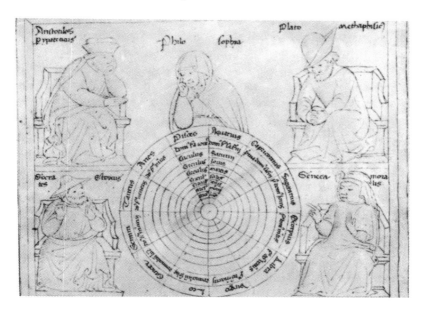

PLATE 19   *Philosophy surrounded by Aristotle, Plato, Socrates, and Seneca
(Bibliothèque nationale)*

Established thus, scholasticism was built into the university framework, with its unique methods of scholarly exposition.

THE EXERCISES: QUESTIO, DISPUTATIO, QUODLIBETICA

The basic scholarly method began with a commentary on a text, the *lectio*, an in-depth study beginning with a grammatical analysis which gave the letter (*littera*), advancing to a logical explanation which provided the meaning (*sensus*), and ending in an exegesis which revealed the text's content of knowledge and thought (*sententia*).

But commentary gave birth to debate. Dialectics enabled one to go beyond the understanding of a text to deal with the issues it raised, and diminished it in the quest for truth. An entire problematics replaced the exegesis. Following the appropriate procedures, the *lectio* developed into the *questio*. The university intellectual was born from the moment he "questioned" the text which then became only a support, when from a passive reader he became an active questioner. The master was no longer an exegete, but a thinker. He gave his solutions, he created. His conclusion of the *questio*, the *determinatio*, was the fruit of his thought.

The *questio* in the thirteenth century was in fact separate from any text. It existed in and of itself. With the active participation of masters and students, it became the object of a debate, it had become the *disputatio*.

Père Mandonnet[3] has given a classic description of it:

> When a master was disputing all the classes given in the morning by the other masters and the bachelors of the faculty ceased; only the master who was disputing gave a short lecture to enable those in attendance to arrive, then the dispute began. It took up a more or less considerable part of the morning. All the bachelors of the faculty and the students of the master who was disputing had to attend the exercise. It seems the other masters and students were free, but there is no doubt that they came in more or less greater numbers depending on the reputation of the master and the object of the dispute. The Parisian clergy as well as prelates and other ecclesiastical figures passing through the capital willingly attended those jousts which thrilled the mind. The *disputatio* was the tournament of clerks.
>
> The question to be disputed was set in advance by the master who was to hold the dispute. It was announced, as was the established day, in the other schools of the faculty . . ..
>
> The dispute was held under the direction of the master, but it was not, strictly speaking, he who debated. It was his bachelor who assumed the role of respondant and thus began his training in these exercises. Objections were usually presented in various ways, first by the masters present, then by the bachelor, and finally, if there was an opportunity, by the students. The bachelor responded to the arguments raised, and when necessary, the master lent him assistance. Such was, in short, the make-up of an

---

[3]   *Revue Thomiste*, 1928, p. 267–9.

ordinary dispute; but that was only the first part of it, although it was the principal one and the most lively.

The objections raised and resolved in the course of the dispute, without a pre-established order, ultimately presented rather disorganized doctrinal material, less similar, however, to the debris on a battlefield than to the half-completed work of a construction site. This is why following that preliminary session there was a second one which bore the name of "magisterial determination."

The first "readable" day, as it was called at that time, that is, the first day that the master who had disputed could give his lecture, for a Sunday, a holiday, or some other obstacle might have prevented it from being the day right after the dispute, the master resumed in his school the subject debated the day before, or a few days earlier. First, he coordinated as much as the subject would allow in an order or a logical succession, the objections raised against his thesis and gave them their definitive formula. He followed those objections with a few arguments in favor of the doctrine he was going to propose. He then went on to a more or less extensive doctrinal exposé of the debated question, which provided the central and essential part of the determination. He concluded by responding to each of the objections raised against the doctrine of his thesis . . ..

The acts of determination, conferred in writing by the master or a listener, form those writings which we call the Disputed Questions, which were the conclusions of the disputation.

Finally, within this framework, a special genre was developed: the *quodlibetica* disputation. Twice a year the masters could hold a session where they made themselves available to deal with a question "raised by anyone on any topic" (*de quolibet ad voluntatem cujuslibet*). Glorieux[4] has described this exercise as follows:

The session began around the hour of terce perhaps, or of sext; rather early, in any event, for it risked going on for a long time. What characterized it, in fact, was its capricious, and impromtu aspect, and the uncertainty which hovered over it. A session of dispute, of argumentation like so many others; but which offered

---

4 *La littérature quodlibétique*, 1936.

this special trait: the initiative was relinquished by the master and was passed on to those in attendance. In ordinary disputes the master announced in advance the subjects that would be covered, he reflected on them and prepared them. In the *quodlibetica* dispute anyone could raise any question. And that was the great danger for the master who was responding. The questions or objections could come from all sides, either hostile or shrewd – anything was possible. He could be questioned in good faith to learn his opinion; but someone might have tried to force him to contradict himself, or to force him to speak on controversial subjects which he would have preferred never to broach. Sometimes it was a curious foreigner, or a worried soul; sometimes a jealous rival or a curious master who would try to put him in an awkward position. Sometimes the questions would be clear and interesting, other times they would be ambiguous and the master would have great difficulty in grasping their exact significance and true meaning. Some would be candidly confined to the purely intellectual realm; others above all had implications of politics or of disparagement . . .. It was thus essential that whoever wanted to hold a *quodlibetica* dispute have an uncommon presence of mind and an almost universal competency.

Thus scholasticism developed, the mistress of rigorous, stimulating, original thought with obedience to the laws of reason. Western thought, which made decisive progress with scholasticism, was forever to remain marked by it. Granted, we are dealing with the vigorous scholasticism of the thirteenth century, led by sharp, demanding minds in full strength. The *flamboyent* scholasticism of the end of the Middle Ages could justifiably inspire the scorn of Erasmus, Luther, and Rabelais. *Baroque* scholasticism inspired the legitimate disgust of Malebranche. But the inspiration and the methodology of scholasticism were incorporated into the progress of Western thought. Descartes, whatever he may have said, owes much to it. In the conclusion of an important book Etienne Gilson writes: "One can understand Cartesianism only by constantly confronting it with that scholasticism it disdains, but at the heart of which it is anchored and by which, through assimilation, one can indeed say it is nourished."

CONTRADICTIONS – HOW TO LIVE: SALARY OR BENEFICE?

Thus armed, the intellectual of the thirteenth century nevertheless remained confronted with many uncertainties, placed in the face of delicate choices. Contradictions arose in the course of a series of university crises.

The first problems were of a material nature. They were profoundly relevant.

The first question was how to live. From the time when the intellectual was no longer a monk whose community assured his survival, he had to earn his living. In the cities the problems of food and lodging, of clothing and equipment – books were expensive – were quite serious. And as time went on the career of a student was all the more costly in that it was so long.

There were two solutions to that problem: a salary or a stipend for the master, and a scholarship or prebend for the student. The salary itself could come from two sources: the master could be paid by his students or by the civil authorities. A scholarship might be the gift of a private benefactor or a grant from a public organization or from a governmental authority.

Associated with these solutions were divergent obligations. The first fundamental option was between a salary and a stipend. In the first case the academic deliberately presented himself as a worker, a producer. In the second case, he did not live off his activity, but could exercise it because he had private means. His entire socioeconomic status was thus defined: a worker or privileged intellectual?

Within the first option others of lesser, but not negligible, importance took shape.

If a master received a salary, he could be a merchant, if his students paid him; or a functionary, if he were remunerated by the communal or princely power; or a sort of domestic, if he lived off the generosity of a benefactor.

As a prebendary he might receive a stipend associated with his intellectual function, which made him a specialized clerk – or be granted a stipend to which were associated other pastoral functions, those of a curé or an abbot, and was thus an intellectual only on the side, indeed, in spite of his ecclesiastical duties.

Beginning in the twelfth century choices were made in part depending upon the time or place, the situation, and the personality of the individual.

We can nevertheless note some general tendencies: for example, masters tended to live off the money they were paid by their students. In this solution they discovered the advantage of being free vis-à-vis temporal authorities: the commune, the prince, the Church, or even a patron. This solution seemed natural to them for it conformed the most with the habits of the urban workplace of which they considered themselves to be members. Masters sold their knowledge and instruction the way artisans sold their wares. They supported that demand for legitimation of which we find so many expressions. The principal one was that all work deserved a salary. This is what confessors' handbooks confirmed: "the master may accept the money of students – the *collecta* – as the price of his work, of his trouble"; which was often recalled by academics, as the doctors of law did in Padua in 1382: "We find it irrational that the worker not profit from his work. Therefore we decree that the doctor who gives the sermon of reply in the name of the college upon a student's reception shall receive from the student in acknowledgement of his work three pounds of cloth and four flasks of wine, or a ducat." Which explains the masters' hunting down students who were lax in paying their fees. The famous law professor at Bologna, Odofredus, wrote: "I will tell you . . . [that] . . . next year I expect to give ordinary lectures well and lawfully as I always have but no extraordinary lectures, for students are not good payers, wishing to learn but not to pay, as the saying is: 'All desire to know but not to pay the price.'"[5]

As for the students, judging from their letters, either authentic or reconstructed as examples in correspondence manuals, they sought above all to be supported by their families or by a benefactor.

---

[5]   Cited in Daly, *The Medieval University*, pp. 155–6. – TRANS.

The Church and especially the papacy took it upon itself to solve that problem. It made a proclamation: there would be free education. The most legitimate of the reasons motivating its decision was a wish to provide education for poor students. Another reason, which reflected an archaic state of mind and referred to the time when there was only strictly religious instruction, held that knowledge was a gift from God and consequently could not be sold, under the threat of simony. Also, teaching was an integral part of the ministry (*officium*) of the clerk. In a famous text St Bernard had denounced the earnings of masters as shameful profit (*turpis questus*).

The papacy thus set forth an entire series of measures. At the time of the Third Lateran Council in 1179, Pope Alexander III proclaimed the principle of free education, and numerous reminders of that decision were made by his successors. At the same time there was to be created near every cathedral church a school whose master would have his livelihood insured by an ecclesiastical stipend.

But in so doing the papacy bound itself with ties of self-interest to the intellectuals who were forced to ask for stipends, and thus stopped, or at least considerably slowed down, the movement which was leading them toward secularity.

The result was that only those who agreed to that material dependence on the Church could be university professors. Certainly, despite the fierce opposton of the Church, lay schools could be established alongside the universities, but instead of dispensing a general education, they were restricted to technical instruction essentially intended for merchants: writing, accounting, foreign languages. Thus the gap between a "liberal" education and technical training was widened. In so doing the Church removed the essential message of Innocent III's opinion as declared in his *Dialogus*:

> Every man endowed with intelligence . . . can fulfill the function of teacher, for through instruction he must lead his brother whom he sees wandering far from the path of truth or morality onto the right path. But the function of preaching, that is, of teaching publicly, belongs only to those who are intended for it, that is, the

bishops and priests in their churches, and the abbots in the monasteries, to whom the care of souls is conferred."

This is a text of primary importance in which a pontiff who was nevertheless not very open to new ideas, recognized, in the face of the general evolution, the distinction that had to be made between the religious function and that of teaching. Undoubtedly this opinion was formed regarding a determined historical context, i.e., an entirely Christian society. But the highest figure in the Church had recognized, at least in those to whom his benefices were distributed, the secular nature of education. As we know, this text has not been developed as it should be.

However, as we will see, in the Middle Ages many masters and students were laymen. They participated no less, however, in the distribution of ecclesiastical benefices, and thus contributed to the worsening of one of the great vices of the Church in the Middle Ages and the Ancien Régime: the allocation of revenues of ecclesiastical benefices to laymen. Moreover the institution of a special benefice for a single master per scholarly center having rapidly proven to be very insufficient, masters and students received ordinary benefices and came to aggravate that other scourge of the Church: the non-residence of the clergy.

The Church's position enhanced the difficulties of those who sought non-ecclesiastical opportunities, notably in civil law and medicine, through education. They often found themselves in ambiguous situations for, if the vogue of legal studies especially continued undiminished, that subject continued to be attacked by eminent ecclesiastics. Roger Bacon declared: "Everything in civil law has a lay character. To address oneself to such a gross art is to leave the Church." Since there could be no official question of them in the universities, a whole group of disciplines which the technical, economic, and social evolution were helping to develop and which were without any immediate religious character, were for centuries in a state of paralysis.

THE QUARREL BETWEEN THE SECULAR MASTERS AND THE MENDICANT ORDERS

A serious crisis, which afflicted the universities in the thirteenth and the beginning of the fourteenth centuries, revealed how ambiguous the intellectuals' situation truly was and how discontent many of them were. This was the quarrel between the secular masters and the regular clergy. The former violently opposed the growing number of masters, members of the new mendicant orders, who were being admitted to the universities.

Indeed, from the start the Dominicans sought to penetrate the universities, the very goal of their founder – preaching and the struggle against the Albigensian heresy – leading them to seek a solid intellectual foundation. The Franciscans soon joined them, as those who on certain points distanced the order from the positions of St Francis (who was hostile to a knowledge in which he saw an obstacle to poverty, privation, and fraternity with the humble) became increasingly influential. At first they were made to feel quite welcome. In 1220 Pope Honorius III congratulated the University of Paris for its acceptance of the Dominicans. Then violent clashes occurred. The University of Paris experienced the most vehement ones, between 1252 and 1290 and particularly during the years 1252–9, 1265–71, and 1282–90. Oxford later suffered from them, between 1303 and 1320, between 1350 and 1360.

The most striking and most typical of these clashes occurred in Paris between 1252 and 1259. It culminated in the William of St-Amour affair. Although complex, it is also informative.

There were five groups of protagonists: the mendicant orders and their Parisian masters, the majority of secular masters at the university, the papacy, the king of France, and the students.

In the thick of the struggle, a secular master, William of St-Amour, published a violent attack against the monks in a treatise entitled "The Perils of the New Age." Condemned by the pope, he was banished despite the strong resistance of a group of academics on his side.

What were the secular masters' grievances against the mendicant orders?

Initially, from the years 1252–4, the grievances were almost exclusively of a corporative nature. The seculars accused the mendicants of violating university statutes. They obtained degrees in theology and taught without first acquiring a masters-of-arts. In 1250 the mendicants obtained from the pope the possibility of receiving, outside the faculty of theology, a license from the chancellor of Notre-Dame; they claimed to have and indeed occupied two chairs, whereas the statutes attributed only one (out of four) to them; and above all they broke university solidarity by continuing to give courses when the university was on strike. They did this in 1229–31, and again in 1253, whereas striking was a right recognized by the papacy and was inscribed in the statutes. Moreover, added the secular masters, the monks were not true academics. They created disloyal competition at the university; they won over students and inspired many to enter a monastic vocation; living off alms, they asked for no money from students as payment for their lectures, and they themselves did not feel bound by the material demands of university life.

Such were the seculars' real grievances; they were legitimate and significant. Academics quickly became aware of the incompatibility of belonging both to an order, however new its style may have become, and to a corporation, however clerical it may have been originally.

Intellectuals who has not received the essential basic training – that given by the faculty of arts – for whom the problem of material sustenance was not raised, and for whom the right to strike meant nothing, were not true intellectuals. They were not scientific workers, because they were not living off their teaching.

Pope Innocent IV yielded to at least part of these arguments: aware of the mendicants' violations of the university statutes, he ordered them to obey these statutes on July 4, 1254, and on the following November 20 restricted the privileges of the orders in his *Etsi animarum* bull.

But his successor Alexander IV, who had been cardinal and was a protector of the Franciscans, revoked the bull of his predecessor on December 22 with the bull *Nec insolitum*, and on

April 14, 1255, with a new bull *Quasi lignum vitae* he confirmed the complete triumph of the mendicants over the secular masters.

The battle took off again, became more intense, and was carried onto another level – no longer corporative, but dogmatic. The secular masters, with William of St-Amour at their head, and writers like Rutebeuf (in poems written for the occasion) and Jean de Meung (in *Le Roman de la Rose*), attacked the mendicant orders at the very foundations of their existence and ideals.

The mendicants were accused of usurping the functions of the clergy: notably in hearing confession and in burials; of being hypocrites who sought out pleasure, riches, and power (the famous *pretender* in the *Roman de la Rose* is a Franciscan); and finally of being heretics: their ideal of evangelical poverty was contrary to the doctrine of Christ and threatened to ruin the Church. This was the polemical argument: as proof, the seculars cited the famous prophesies of Joachim of Fiore, quite in fashion among some Franciscans, who announced the beginning in the year 1260 of a new age in which the current Church would cede its place to a new Church where poverty would be the rule. The development of Joachim's ideas by the Franciscan Gerard of Borgo San Donnino in his *Introduction to the Eternal Gospel*, published in 1254, provided ammunition for the seculars.

The seculars were no doubt exaggerating. The slander and maneuvers which aimed only to shower discredit upon the mendicant orders tarnished their cause. On the basic issues St Bonaventure and St Thomas Aquinas himself, whom one cannot suspect of having hostility towards the university, were able to agree.

Thus the affair had its destructive aspects. Most of the popes, only too happy to take a side which gave satisfaction to the orders which were completely devoted to them, and which at the same time fettered the secular academics even more, shattered the resistance of the seculars. The king of France, St Louis, completely devoted to the Franciscans, allowed this to continue: Rutebeuf reproached him bitterly for being a puppet in the mendicants' hands, and for not defending his kingdom to which the rights of the university were of the greatest importance. The students seem to have hesitated; many were aware of the advantages of the mendicants' teaching, and even more of the brilliance of their personalities and the novelty of certain aspects of their doctrine: a paradox which confused the affair and obscured it in the eyes of historians.

The new spirit was divided between the two sides in this struggle. On the one hand, the mendicants were strangers to the corporative aspect which was at the foundation of the intellectual movement; at its social and economic foundations they destroyed the hope of a new class of intellectual workers; but, settled in an urban environment, close to the new classes, they knew better their own intellectual and spiritual needs. Scholasticism did not have any more brilliant representatives than some of their members; it was a Dominican, St Thomas Aquinas, who carried it to its heights. Through the compromise at the end of his pontificate, Innocent IV might have kept the mendicants' inspiration within the university corporation, which would have remained the mistress of its destiny. His successors were unable to do so.

But in its new form the struggle revealed all that the university spirit had against an important aspect of the monastic ideal,

Un dominicain enseignant.
(Miniature du 3e livre de Vincent de Beauvais).

PLATE 20   *A Dominican teaching (miniature from the third book of Vincent of Beauvais) (Courtesy Giraudon)*

which was taken up, revitalized, but also carried to its heights by the mendicants.

The issue of poverty was indeed a central one which divided everyone involved. Poverty resulted from that asceticism which was a refusal of the world, a pessimism with regard to man and nature. In this, already, it clashed with the humanist and naturalist optimism of the majority of intellectuals. But, above all, poverty for the Dominicans and Franciscans inevitably led to the need for begging. Here, the intellectuals' opposition was absolute. In their opinion one could earn a living only from one's work. In this respect they were expressing the attitude of all workers of the age, who, whatever may have been said, were largely hostile to the new orders because of their begging. The message of St Dominic and St Francis of Assisi was obliterated. It was difficult to promote an ideal condition which so resembled the poverty which an entire working population was seeking to avoid. As Jean de Meung says:

> I can swear to you without delay that it is not written in any law, at least not in ours, that Jesus Christ or his apostles, while they went about on earth, were ever seen seeking their bread, for they did not wish to beg. The masters of divinity in the city of Paris were formerly accustomed to preach thus . . . a capable man, if he doesn't have the means by which he may live, should seek his living by laboring with his own hands, his own body, no matter how religious or eager to serve God he may be . . .. St Paul ordered the apostles to work in order to recover what they needed to live on, and he forbade them to beg, saying, "work with your hands; never acquire anything through another."[6]

Carried to this level the quarrel expanded into a battle between the secular masters in general and the regular clergy. University issues then held only a secondary place. However, the Parisian masters – who had lost so much in the affair and who, even if they had not always fought with good weapons, had fought for the very definition of their individuality – had to hear at the

---

[6]   Jean de Meung, *The Romance of the Rose*, translated by Charles Dahlberg (Princeton University Press, 1983), pp. 198–9. – Trans.

PLATE 21   *Boniface VIII (Courtesy Giraudon)*

Paris Council of 1290 these violent words of the papal legate, Cardinal Benoit Gaetani, the future Boniface VIII:

I would like to see here all the Parisian masters whose stupidity shines in this city. With mad presumption and guilty boldness they have arrogated the right to interpret the privilege in question. Do they imagine that the Roman curia could grant a privilege of this importance without reflection? Were they therefore unaware that the Roman curia did not have feet of feathers, but of lead? All these masters imagine that they have a huge reputation as scholars among us; on the contrary, we judge them to be fools among fools, they who have infected both themselves and the entire world with the poison of their doctrine . . . . It is not admissible that any privilege of the Holy See might be reduced to nothing by the quibbles of the masters.

Masters of Paris, you have made your entire science and doctrine ridiculous, and continue to do so . . . . Since the Christian world has been committed to us, we must take into account, not what might please your whims as clerks, but what is of use to the entire Christian world. You perhaps believe that you hold a great reputation among us; but we consider your glory to be only foolishness and smoke . . . . Under the penalty of being deprived of offices and benefices, we forbid, by virtue of obedience, all masters henceforth to preach, debate, or determine, in public or in private, the privilege of monks . . . . The court of Rome, rather than revoking the privilege, will crush the University of Paris. We have not been called upon by God to acquire knowledge or to shine in the eyes of men, but to save our souls. And because the conduct and the doctrine of the brothers save many souls, the privilege that has been conferred upon them will always be preserved.[7]

Did not the university masters save souls? Did their teaching deserve such insults? The future Boniface VIII already knew how to stir up enmity.

---

[7] This text is cited by Mgr Glorieux in an article entitled "Prélats Français contre religieux mendiants – Autour de la bulle *Ad fructus uberes* (1281–1290)," which appeared in the *Revue d'Histoire de l'Eglise de France*, 1925. Mgr Glorieux distinguishes three phases: university opposition (1252–9); doctrinal opposition (1265–71); and episcopal opposition (1282–90).

THE CONTRADICTIONS OF SCHOLASTICISM:
THE DANGER OF IMITATING THE ANCIENTS

Also serious, and frought with crises, were the contradictions of the scholastic spirit.

A rational way of thinking, but based on ancient thought, it was not always able to go beyond that thought, to transpose the problems of an outdated historical context into a current one. St Thomas himself was sometimes a prisoner of Aristotle. There was nevertheless a contradiction in seeking an explanation for Christianity and its adaptation to the needs of the time with the help of doctrines dating before Christianity itself.

There are numerous examples of this, three of which we will now examine.

As we have attempted to show, nothing was more essential for academics than to define the issues of work, from the time they presented themselves as workers. But for the ancients work was essentially manual labor, the work of slaves, the exploitation of whom enabled ancient societies to live, a work which was consequently despised. St Thomas adopted Aristotle's theory of servile work, and Rutebeuf, the poorest of the student-poets, proudly proclaimed: "I am not a manual worker." Scholasticism was unable to make a place for manual labor – a most serious problem, for in isolating the privileged work of the intellectual, it consented to undermine the foundations of the university condition, while it separated the intellectual from the other workers with whom he was connected in the urban workplace.

A profession of intellectual audacity, of impassioned curiosity, the intellectual profession, although it was essential to temper its extravagances, had nothing to gain by borrowing a morality of mediocrity from the ancients, one which from the μςǫςῆ χςχῆ of the Greeks had derived the *aurea mediocritas* (the golden mean) of Horace. It was, however, a morality of the happy medium, a sign of a bourgeois mentality and of petty renunciation, which it often lauded: "The man who claims to have nothing," says *Le Roman de la Rose*, "provided he has enough to live from day to day, he is content with his earnings, and does not think he is lacking anything . . .. The name of the mean is sufficiency. There lies the abundance of virtues." The narrowing of horizons, the death of just ambitions.

In the dynamic world of the thirteenth century, in which scholasticism was harmoniously building its intellectual edifice, it happened that it was unable to detach itself from the ancient theory of art as the imitation of nature, which disregarded and hindered the creation of human work. As Jean de Meung again says:

> [Art] does not make her forms as true, however, with very attentive care, she kneels before Nature and like a truant beggar, poor in knowledge and force, she begs and requests and asks of her. She struggles to follow her so that Nature may wish to teach her how with her ability she may properly subsume all creatures in her figures. She also watches how Nature works, for she would like very much to perform such a work, and she imitates her like a monkey. But her sense is so bare and feeble that she cannot make living things, no matter how newborn they seem.[8]

Here, alas, is art which was readying itself to become photography.

THE TEMPTATIONS OF NATURALISM

Scholasticism sought ties between God and Nature; but the naturalism of the intellectuals developed in many directions. The goliardic tradition, still lively in the universities, was carried on, truculent, with less aggressiveness but more self-assurance. Nature and genius were not content to groan for Jean de Meung as they did for Alan of Lille. The second part of the *Roman de la Rose* is a hymn to the inexhaustible fertility of Nature, an impassioned invitation to unreservedly obey its laws, an appeal to a frenzied sexuality. Marriage is treated roughly in it. The limitations marriage imposes are stigmatized as being against nature in the same degree as sodomy: "Marriage is a detestable

---

[8]   *The Romance of the Rose*, trans. Charles Dahlberg, pp. 271–2.

bond . . .. Nature is not so stupid that she has Marotte born only for Robichon, if we put our wits to work, nor Robichon only for Marietta or Agnes or Perette. Instead, fair son, never doubt that she has made all women for all men and all men for all women."[9] Then there is the famous, completely Rabelaisian flight of fancy:

> For God's sake, my lords, you who live, take care not to follow such people. At the works of Nature, be quicker than any squirrel, lighter and more mobile than a bird or the wind may be. Do not lose this good pardon; provided that you work well at this, I pardon you all your sins. Move, skip, leap; don't let yourself get cold or let your limbs become tepid. Put all your tools to work; he who works well keeps warm enough.
>
> Plow, for God's sake, my barons, plow and restore your lineages. Unless you think on plowing vigorously, there is nothing that can restore them. Tuck up your clothes in front, as though to take the air; or if you please, be quite bare, but don't get too cold or too hot. With your two hands bare raise the guideboards of your plows . . .[10]

The rest altogether defies decency.

This overflowing vitality overcomes the enemy, death. But man, like the phoenix, is always reborn. There are always survivors of the ride with the Grim Reaper:

> Thus, if Death devours the phoenix, the phoenix still remains alive; if it had devoured a thousand, the phoenix would remain. It is the phoenix in its ideal common form that Nature reshapes into individuals; and this common form would be entirely lost if the next phoenix were not left alive. All things under the circle of the moon have this very same mode of being, so that if one of them can remain, its species so lives in it that Death can never catch up with it.[11]

In Nature's challenge to Death, in that epic poem of ever reborn humanity, in that vitalism *à la Diderot*, where is the

9 Ibid., p. 238.
10 Ibid., p. 324.
11 Ibid., p. 271.

Christian spirit, what place is made for the *Memento quia pulvis es et in pulverem reverteris* [Remember that you are dust and will return to dust]?

It is a naturalism which might also be developed into a theory of society *à la Rousseau*. In his description of the golden age and the iron age which followed, Jean de Meung turns all social hierarchy, every social order, into an evil which replaced the joy of primitive equality in which ownership did not exist:

> Then they had to seek out someone who would guard their dwellings, catch wrongdoers, and give justice to complainants without anyone daring to contradict him. Therefore they assembled to elect someone.
>
> They elected a great scoundrel among them, the one who was largest, with the strongest back and limbs, and made him their prince and lord. He swore that he would maintain justice for them and would protect their dwellings if each one individually were to hand over to him enough goods to enable him to support himself. They agreed thus among themselves as he suggested, and he held this office for a long time. When the robbers, full of malice, saw him alone, they got together and beat him on many occasions when they came to steal. Then the people had to assemble again and urge, each one for himself, that the prince be given sergeants. Then, collectively, they taxed themselves and gave him tribute, revenues, and large holdings of land. From this source, according to the writings of the ancients, arose the first kings and earthly princes; for we know the deeds of the ancients by the writings that we have, and we should give them thanks and praise for what they have left.[12]

THE DIFFICULT BALANCE OF FAITH AND REASON: ARISTOTELIANISM AND AVERROISM

Were the intellectuals of the thirteenth century able to maintain another balance, that of faith and reason? This was the whole adventure of Aristotelianism in the thirteenth century. For if Aristotle indeed signified something other than the rational

---

[12] *Ibid.*, p. 172.

spirit, and if scholastic reason was fed from other sources than the Stagirite, it was around him that the game was played.

The Aristotle of the thirteenth century was different from the one of the twelfth century. First, he was more complete. To the logician known primarily in the twelfth century was added, thanks to a new generation of translators, the physicist, the moralist of *Nichomachean Ethics*, and the metaphysician. He was then interpreted. He arrived accompanied by the commentaries of the great Arab philosophers, Avicenna and especially Averroës. They pushed him to the extreme, and distanced him as far as was possible from Christianity.

There was not one, but at least two Aristotles who made their way into Western Europe: the true Aristotle, and the one belonging to Averroës. There were more, in fact, because each commentator, or almost each, had *his own* Aristotle. But two tendencies in this movement stand out: that of the great Dominican doctors, Albert the Great and Thomas Aquinas, who wanted to reconcile Aristotle with the Scriptures, and that of the Averroists who, wherever they saw contradiction, accepted it and wanted to follow both Aristotle and the Scriptures. They thus invented the doctrine of the "double truth":

> One truth is that of revelation . . . the other is only that of simple philosophy and natural reason. When a conflict arises we will therefore simply say: here are the conclusions to which my reason as a philosopher leads me, but because God cannot lie, I adhere to the truth he has revealed to us and I cling to it through faith.

Whereas Albert the Great declared: "If someone believes that Aristotle is a god, that man must believe he is not mistaken. But if he is convinced that Aristotle is a man, there is no doubt that he could be as mistaken as we are." Whereas St Thomas was persuaded that Averroës "was not so much a Peripatetic as a corrupter of peripatetic philosophy," and Siger of Brabant, the head of the Averroists, asserted: "I say that Aristotle completed the sciences, because none who have followed him up to our time, that is, for close to 1,500 years, has been able to add anything to his writings, nor find an error of any importance in them . . .. Aristotle is a divine being." There was strong opposition to the Alberto-Thomist Aristotelianism, as well as to Averroism. It was led by the Augustinians who set Plato's authority against that of Aristotle. But although St Augustine was one of the great sources of scholasticism, neo-Augustinianism leaning on Platonism encountered the determined hostility of the great scholastics. For them the metaphorical thought of the Academician posed a great danger for true philosophy. As Albert the Great wrote:

> Most of the time, when Aristotle refutes the opinions of Plato, he does not refute the essence, but the form. In fact, Plato had a bad method of exposition. Everything is figured in his writings and his teachings are metaphorical, and he places things behind words that are other than what they mean, as, for example, when he says that the soul is a circle.

Thomism was opposed to that confusing way of thinking and throughout the century – and for centuries – the Augustinians and the Platonists battled all rational innovations, and defended conservative positions. Their great tactic in the thirteenth century was to impair Aristotle's authority using Averroës, and St Thomas's using Aristotle, and hence Averroës. Through the intermediary of Averroism Thomism was always the primary target.

The century was riddled by anti-Aristotelian attacks, which were only so many university crises.

In 1210 the teaching of Aristotle's *Physics* and *Metaphysics* was forbidden at the University of Paris. The ban was renewed by the Holy See in 1215 and 1228. However, upon its founding in 1229 the very orthodox University of Toulouse, to attract students, made it known that the books forbidden in Paris would be taught there. In truth, the bans remained a dead letter in Paris. The condemned books appeared on the programs of study. The admirable Thomist construction seemed to have solved all problems; the Averroist crisis once again put everything into question. A certain number of masters of the faculty of arts, at the head of which was Siger of Brabant and Boethius of

PLATE 22   *Averroës conversing with Porphyrius (Courtesy Giraudon)*

Dacia, taught the most extreme theses of the Philosopher – Aristotle had become the philosopher *par excellence*
– learned through Averroës. Besides the "double truth" they
taught the eternity of the world – which denied creation – refused to admit that God was the efficient cause of things
but was only the final cause, and denied Him the foreknowledge
of contingent futures. Finally some – it is doubtful that Siger was
included here – asserted the unity of the intellect as an agent,
which denied the existence of the individual soul.

As of 1270 the Bishop of Paris, Etienne Tempier, had condemned the Averroists, and St Thomas was eager to keep his
distance by in turn attacking them avidly. After St Thomas's
death in 1274 a large offensive was launched against Aristotelianism. It culminated in the double condemnation pronounced
in 1277 by Etienne Tempier, and by the archbishop of Canterbury, Robert Kilwardby.

PLATE 23   *St Thomas crushing Averroës (Courtesy Giraudon-Anderson)*

PLATE 24   *St Augustine crushing Aristotle (Musée de Besançon)*

Etienne Tempier had compiled a list of 219 propositions condemned as heretical. It was a true amalgam. In addition to strictly Averroist theses, some twenty propositions more or less directly touched upon the teaching of Thomas Aquinas, and others targeted opinions offered in extremist milieux, heirs of the goliards, some of which had contaminated the Averroists:

18 – That the future resurrection must not be admitted by the philosopher, because it is impossible to examine the problem rationally;

152 – That theology is based on fables;

155 – That one must not be concerned with burial;

168 – That continence is not in itself a virtue;

169 – That total abstinence from the work of the flesh corrupts virtue and the species;

174 – That the Christian law has its fables and errors like other religions;

175 – Which is an obstacle to learning;

176 – That happiness is found in this life, and not in another.

This "syllabus" incited strong reactions. The Dominican order took no notice of it. Giles of Rome declared: "One must not be concerned with them, for those propositions were not made upon the convocation of all the Parisian masters, but at the request of a few narrow minded men."

A secular master in the faculty of theology, Godfrey of Fontaine, launched a detailed and pitiless critique of the syllabus. He demanded the suppression of the absurd articles whose condemnations would impede intellectual progress, of those on which people could have different opinions.

Although the condemnations earned little respect, they ruined the Averroist party. Siger of Brabant undoubtedly ended up miserably. The end of his life is cloaked in mystery. Imprisoned in Italy, it is believed he was assassinated there. This enigmatic figure entered into glory thanks to Dante who put him in Paradise next to St Thomas and St Bonaventure:

> Essa è la luce eterna di Sigieri
> Che, leggendo nel vico degli strami,
> Silloggizzò indiviosi veri.

(That is the eternal light of Siger/who in his teaching in the Rue du Fouarre/put truths which displeased into syllogisms.)

The truth is that Siger, very little known, represented a milieu that was even less well known, which was, at a certain time, the very soul of the University of Paris.

In fact he expressed the opinion of the majority of the faculty of arts which, despite what has been said, was the salt and yeast of the university, and which often left its mark on it.

Basic instruction was obtained in that faculty where due to the large number of academics there sprung forth the most impassioned discussions, the boldest curiosity, and the most fertile exchanges. In that faculty one encountered the poor clerks who would not continue long enough to obtain the license, let alone the costly doctorate, but who animated debates with their anxious questions. One was closest there to the people of the cities, to the exterior world; in the faculty of arts there was the least concern with obtaining prebends or with displeasing the ecclesiastical hierarchy; there was the liveliest lay spirit, and its academics were among the freest. It was there that Aristotelianism bore all its fruit. It was there that one mourned, as an irreparable loss, the death of Thomas Aquinas, and it was the "artists" who, in a moving letter, asked the Dominican order to give them the mortal remains of the great doctor. The illustrious theologian had been one of their own.

PLATE 25 *A doctoral examination*

It was in the Averroist camp of the faculty of arts that the most rigorous ideal of the intellectual was conceived.

Boethius of Dacia asserted that "the *philosophers*" – as the intellectuals called themselves – "are naturally virtuous, chaste, and temperate, righteous, strong and liberal, sweet and magnanimous, magnificent, subject to laws, detached from the attraction of pleasures . . ." – those same intellectuals who in his time were persecuted "out of malice, envy, ignorance, and stupidity."

Magnanimous. There is the great word uttered. As Gauthier has admirably shown, it was in those intellectuals that one finds the supreme ideal of magnanimity which for Abelard was already a virtue of initiative, a *passionate optimism.* It was

> enthusiasm for human tasks, energy in their strength as men, confidence in human techniques which, in the service of man's strength, were alone capable of insuring the success of human tasks. [It was a] typically secular spirituality, made for men who remain active in the world, and seek God, but no longer immediately like monastic spirituality, but through man and through the world.[13]

THE RELATIONSHIP BETWEEN REASON AND EXPERIENCE

Other reconciliations were equally difficult to achieve: that between reason and experience, and between theory and practice.

The English school with the help of the great scholar Robert Grosseteste, the chancellor of Oxford and bishop of Lincoln, then with a Franciscan group from Oxford out of which Roger Bacon emerged, attempted the former. Roger Bacon defined their program in his *Opus Majus*:

---

[13]   R. A. Gautier, *Magnanimité: L'idéal de la grandeur dans la philosophie paienne et dans la théologie chrétienne* (Paris: Vrin, 1951).

PLATE 26 *The clerk, the astronomer, and the computist (Bibliothèque
nationale)*

The Latins have laid the foundations of knowledge regarding languages, mathematics, and perspective; I want now to turn to the foundations provided by experimental science, for without experience one cannot know anything fully . . .. If someone who has never seen fire proves through reasoning that fire burns, changes things and destroys them, the mind of his listener will not be satisfied with that, and will not avoid fire before he has placed his hand or something combustible on the fire, to prove through experience what his reasoning had taught him. But once it has had the experience of combustion the mind is assured and rests in the light of truth. Thus reasoning is not enough – one needs experience.

In this the demise of scholasticism was foreseen; the balance was ready to be upset, empiricism was breaking through.

THE RELATIONSHIP BETWEEN THEORY AND PRACTICE

It was physicians, and with them, surgeons and opticians, who asserted the necessary connection between theory and practice.

Averroës said: "Surgery which is learned through practice alone, and which is practiced without previous study, like the surgery of peasants and of all illiterate folk, is a purely mechanical undertaking, is not truly theoretical, and is truly neither a science nor an art." But on the other hand he specifies: "Following theoretical studies the physician must avidly engage in practical exercises. Lessons and dissertations teach only a small part of surgery and anatomy. Indeed, there is very little in these two sciences which can be represented through words."

But was not scholasticism close to falling into one of its major temptations – abstraction?

Its language, Latin, although it remained a living language since it was able to adapt to the needs of the learning of the times and one could express all new things in it, was deprived of the richness of the rapidly developing vernacular tongues, and distanced the intellectuals from the lay masses and their problems, their psychology.

PLATE 27 *First representation of a person wearing glasses (Musée de Besançon)*

Attached to abstract and eternal truths, the scholastic risked losing contact with history, with what was contingent, moving, evolving. When St Thomas said "the goal of philosophy is not to know what men have thought, but rather the truth of things," he in fact rejects a philosophy which would only be a history of philosophic thought; but was he not amputating a dimension from thought?

One of the great pitfalls of the scholastic intellectuals was that of forming an intellectual technocracy. Indeed, at the end of the thirteenth century the university masters monopolized the high ecclesiastical and lay positions. They were bishops, archdeacons, canons, advisors, government ministers. It was the age of doctors, theologians, and jurists. A university freemasonry dreamt of controlling western Christian Europe. It proclaimed along with Jean de Meung and Boethius of Dacia that 'the intellectual is more than a prince, more than a king." Roger Bacon, aware that learning should be a collective effort, and who dreamt of a huge team of scholars, also hoped that academics would direct the destinies of the world alongside temporal leaders. He implored the pope to undertake the formation of that directing group. Regarding the comet of 1264 which foretold of plagues and wars, he proclaimed: "How useful it would have been to the Church if the quality of the sky, at that time, had been discovered by scholars and communicated through them to prelates and princes . . .. There would not have been such slaughtering of Christians nor so many souls driven to Hell."

A pious wish that was hiding a fearsome utopia. It was also necessary to say to the intellectual: *sutor, ne supra* . . .[14] If it is true that knowledge culminates in politics, it is rarely good that scholars end up as politicians.

---

[14] "*Sutor, ne supra crepidam*" is the Latin of a remark made by the Greek painter Apelles (4th cent. BC) when a shoemaker criticized the sandals in his painting and then, looking up, began to critique the rest of the painting – "Shoemaker, no higher than the sandals." – TRANS.

3

FROM ACADEMIC TO HUMANIST

The end of the Middle Ages was a period of transformation; the halt of demographic development, then its decline, made worse by famines and plagues (the one of 1348 was catastrophic), and disruptions in the supply of precious metals to Western economies which produced a famine of silver then of gold rendered even worse by wars – the Hundred Years War, the War of the Roses, the Iberian and Italian wars – hastened the transformation of the economic and social structures of Western Europe. The evolution of the feudal rent system which overwhelmingly took on a monetary form upset social conditions. The gap was widening between the victims and the beneficiaries of that evolution. The dividing line passed in the midst of the urban classes. While in certain places (Flanders, northern Italy, large cities) the more harshly exploited artisanry displayed signs of proletarianism and joined the lot of the peasantry, the upper levels of the urban bourgeoisie, which derived its resources both from an on-going pre-capitalist activity and from land revenues it was able to secure for itself, joined forces with the former ruling classes: the nobility, the regular clergy, and the high secular clergy, who on the whole succeeded in turning a compromising situation around in their favor. Political factors played a major role in this turning around. Political power came to the aid of economic powers. It would support the Ancien Régime for centuries. This was the age of the Prince. It was by

PLATE 28　*St Jerome, By Dürer (Bibliotèque nationale)*

serving him, by making oneself his functionary or his courtier that one became rich, powerful, and prestigious. The powerful ancients understood this when they joined forces with tyrannies and monarchies, while new men, through the favor of the prince, slid in among them.

In this context the intellectual of the Middle Ages was to disappear. The front of the cultural stage would be taken over by a new character – the humanist. But it was only at the end that the latter would give the push which caused his predecessor to disappear. The medieval intellectual was not assassinated; he volunteered for that death and that metamorphosis. Through their abjurations, the great majority of academics throughout the fourteenth and fifteenth centuries prepared for the disappearance of the medieval intellectual.

THE EVOLUTION OF THE LIVES OF ACADEMICS

The academics at the end of the Middle Ages made a definitive choice between belonging to the working world and being integrated into privileged groups. For centuries there was no longer an intellectual worker in Western Europe. Or rather, only obscure teachers in communal schools could have been given that name, those who, even if some of them played a role in revolutionary movements like the Revolt of the Ciompi in Florence in 1378, did not occupy an important place in the intellectual movement.

Academics in the fourteenth and fifteenth centuries certainly did not abandon the resources they could derive from salaried work. On the contrary, they held fiercely to those meager profits in difficult times. With increased avidity they demanded that their students pay for their lessons – a practice which the Church was unable to eradicate completely. They reinforced the stipulations which defined the gifts the students owed the masters at the time of exams. They restricted all university expenditures which could be made at their expense. By ordinance the number of poor students who received instruction and a degree without paying rapidly declined. In Padua at the beginning of the fifteenth century there was no longer more than one non-paying student per faculty: a token measure which safeguarded the principle defended by the Church. It was the equivalent of the contribution to God which the rich merchant took from his profit to give to the poor.

At the same time there was a decline in the number of students of modest condition fed into the universities, and they had previously been the fodder of the faculties. Henceforth there arrived only those whom a protector supported in order to strictly control them, or those who were content with a bohemian existence in which intellectual ambitions were secondary – a Villon, for example.

A curious decision made by the doctors of civil law in Padua illustrates this evolution in the relationship between masters and students. An addition to the statutes dating from 1400 instituted a sliding scale of university taxes levied to the benefit of the masters, whereas the students receiving scholarships saw their funds held at a fixed rate. As a result, university politics entered into a general phase which was manifest throughout Western Europe in the second half of the fourteenth century. Faced with a rise in prices, administrative authorities and employers attempted to block salaries, admitting no connection between the cost of living and the remunerations which could lead to the establishment of a sliding scale of salaries, whereas the beneficiaries of unearned income, of rent, of leases tried, often successfully, to adapt their revenues to the cost of living, either by payments in kind or by a transferal into real money of payments made on account.

This example shows that academics joined the social groups living off income of a feudal or seigneurial or capitalist nature.

It was moreover from income of that kind that academics derived most of their resources. First their were ecclesiastical benefices, and then the investment of capital in property: houses and land. The chartulary of the University of Bologna enables us to follow the establishment, notably at the end of the thirteenth century, of considerable university fortunes. Masters – this was true especially for the most famous who earned more, but it remained true to a lesser degree for most of them – became rich landowners. Following the example of other rich people, they moreover took part in speculative activities. They turned into usurers. They primarily made loans with interest to needy students, and most often held those objects of double value to them – their books – as collateral.

Francesco Accorso owned property in Budrio, in Olmetola, a splendid villa in Riccardiana with a hydraulic wheel which at that time was a wonder. In Bologna he owned jointly with his brothers a beautiful house with a tower which forms the current right wing of the Palazzi Comunale. Along with other doctors he formed a commercial enterprise for the sale of books in Bologna and abroad. He engaged in usury on such a large scale that on his deathbed he had to ask for absolution from Pope Nicholas IV, who granted it to him, as was the custom.

The same was true of Alberto d'Odofredo, the son of the great Odofredo, who was a usurer *non paeciol, ma sovrano* (not small, but royal), who in addition to many land holdings, held an interest in a linen company.

In 1326 the master Giovanni d'Andrea gave his daughter Novella with a dowry of 600 gold bolognini, which was a considerable sum at that time.

But that income was caught up in the depreciation of feudal and land revenue following their conversion into money and the

PLATE 29 *Francesco Accorso (Bibliothèque nationale)*

monetary vicissitudes at the end of the Middle Ages, which was stricken with devaluations and crises. The wealth of many academics was lost; houses and land were sold one after the other. Which explains the eagerness to collect other income: student fees and exam salaries. It also explains the replenishment, based on economic considerations, of a portion of the university personnel. It finally explains the reasons of a financial nature which pushed the academics toward the new centers of wealth, toward the courts of princes and into the entourages of ecclesiastical and secular patrons.

TOWARD A HEREDITARY ARISTOCRACY

However, the replenishment of that personnel was in part stifled by the tendency of academics to recruit each other hereditarily. Already in the thirteenth century the famous Italian legal scholar Accorso had proclaimed preferential rights for the sons of doctors to the succession of vacant chairs in Bologna. But the commune had prevented that in 1295, 1299, and 1304. They were measures taken in vain, however. When in 1397 new statutes of the college of jurists stipulated the promotion of only a single Bolognese citizen per year to the doctorate, the sons, brothers, and nephews of doctors were exempt from that stipulation. They, on the contrary, were accorded many places. In Padua the free admission into the college of jurists for any doctor belonging to the masculine lineage of a doctor, even if one of the intervening ancestors had not been a doctor himself, was decreed in 1394. In 1409 it was specified that the son of a doctor was to take his exams free of charge. This formation of a university oligarchy, while it contributed to singularly lowering the prevailing intellectual level, conferred one of the essential characteristics of nobility upon the university milieu: heredity. It turned that milieu into a caste.

To transform themselves into an aristocracy, academics adopted one of the usual means employed by groups and individuals wanting to rub shoulders with the nobility, as Marc Bloch has admirably pointed out: they adopted an aristocratic mode of life.

They turned their dress and the emblems of their function into symbols of nobility. The chair which was increasingly placed on a dais of seigneurial grandeur, separated them, placed them higher up, magnified them. The golden ring and the beret, which they were given on the day of the *conventus publicus* and the *inceptio*, were less insignias of a function, and increasingly emblems of prestige. They wore the long robe, the vair hood, often an ermine collar, and over everything those long gloves which in the Middle Ages were the symbol of social rank and power. Statutes demanded that candidates provide an increasing number of gloves for the doctors at the time of their exams. A Bolognese text of 1387 specifies:

Before receiving his doctorate, the candidate will be expected to place at the given time into the hands of the beadle a sufficient number of gloves for all the doctors of the college . . .. These gloves will be long and full enough to cover the hand to the middle of the arm. They will be of good chamois leather and large enough so that the hands can fit into them with ease and comfort. By good chamois leather it is understood that they will be of the kind that is bought for at least 23 sous per dozen.

Doctoral celebrations were increasingly accompanied with festivals such as were held by nobles: balls, theater productions, jousts.

The homes of academics became luxurious and those of the richest, such as Accorso, were flanked by the towers theoretically reserved for the nobility. Their tombs were veritable monuments, like those which still decorate the churches of Bologna, or were even erected outdoors.

The rectors of Bologna were soon statutorily expected to lead an aristocratic life, and among them one encountered members of the ducal family of Burgundy and the marquisate family of Baden. They received the right to bear arms and to be accompanied by an escort of five men.

The "artists," who were less respected, nevertheless obtained the privilege of not doing military service, and students, if they were rich enough, could find a replacement to serve for them.

A significant evolution occurred in the title of "master." At the beginning, in the twelfth century, the *magister* was a foreman, the head of the workshop. The school master was a master like other artisans. His title indicated his function on the workplace. It soon became a title of glory. Already Adam du Petit Pont snubbed a cousin who from the heart of the English countryside wrote to him in Paris without greeting him with the coveted title. A thirteenth-century text states: "Masters do not teach to be useful, but to be called *Rabbi*," that is, lords, according to the text of the Gospel. In the fourteenth century *magister* became the equivalent of *dominus*, or lord.

In documents the masters of Bologna were called *nobiles viri et primarii cives* – "noble men and principal citizens" – and in every-day life, *domini legum*, "the jurist lords." Students called their favorite master *dominus meus*, "my lord," and this title evoked ties of vassalage. Even a grammarian, Mino del Colle, declared to his students: "The much sought-after acquisition of knowledge is worth more than any other treasure; it pulls the poor out of their dust, it ennobles the non-noble, and confers an illustrious reputation upon him, and enables the nobles to go beyond the non-nobles by belonging to an elite."

Thus again knowledge became a possession and a treasure, an instrument of power and no longer a disinterested end in itself.

As Huizinga has noted with such perspicacity, at its decline the Middle Ages tended to establish an equivalence chivalry/ learning, to give the title of doctor the same rights as to that of knight:

> "Learning, Faith, and Chivalry" are the three flowers of the *Chapel des Fleurs-de-lis* of Philippe de Vitri . . . (1335) and it is said in *Le Livre des Faicts du Maréschal Boucicault*: "Two things have, by the will of God, been established in the world, like two pillars to sustain the order of divine and human laws . . .. These two flawless pillars are Chivalry and Learning, which go very well together."[1]

---

[1]   J. Huizinga, *The Waning of the Middle Ages: A Study of the forms of Life, Thought, and Art in France and The Netherlands in the XIVth and XVth Centuries* (London: Edward Arnold & Co., 1948), p. 55. – TRANS.

In 1391 Froissart distinguished between knights in arms and *knights in laws*. The emperor Charles IV had conferred a knighthood on Bartolus, and the right to bear arms for Bohemia. At the end of this evolution Francis I in 1533 conferred knighthood on the doctors of the university.

We can understand that the academics who had become so eminent would no longer run the risk of being confused with other workers. That would have been to renounce nobility by virtue of the principle of derogation, so strong above all in France where Louis XI fought in vain against it. The intellectuals shared the opinion once again holding manual labor in profound contempt, which in the time of humanism, as Henri Hauser has well pointed out, was worsened by prejudices fed on Greco-Latin literature. One was henceforth far from the drive

PLATE 30   *St Cosma and St Damian in doctors' robes (Bibliothèque de la Sorbonne)*

which in the cities of the twelfth and thirteenth centuries drew the liberal and the mechanical arts together into a common dynamic unity. Thus the divorce between theory and practice, science and technology, which threatened scholasticism, was ultimately accomplished. This was especially true among physicians. There was a separation of the physician/clerk and the apothecary/spicer, the surgeon. In fourteenth-century France a series of edicts and ordinances sanctioned the distinction made between surgeons, the first edict being from Philip the Fair in 1311. Henceforth one distinguished the "long-robed surgeons" who held the bachelor degree or license by virtue of statutes, the first known of which date from 1379, and who formed a surgical aristocracy, from the barber-surgeons who shaved heads and practiced minor surgery, sold ointments and teas, bled, dressed wounds and contusions, and opened sores. They were grouped into two different confraternities – religion was modeled on society – that of Saints Cosma and Damian for the first group, and that of the Holy Sepulcher for the second. We can imagine the handicap that was placed on scientific progress by the division established between the world of scholars and the world of practitioners, the scientific and the technical worlds.

THE COLLEGES AND THE ENNOBLING OF THE UNIVERSITIES

This ennobling of the university is also noted in the development of colleges, a development which should be reviewed in proper perspective. As charitable foundations, the colleges at first only accepted a very small minority of privileged students, and were not the centers of studies they have been reputed to be. Later, although some of them monopolized certain areas of study to the point that the college established in 1257 by Robert de Sorbon was ultimately confused with the faculty of theology and gave its name to the University of Paris, and although the universities of Oxford and Cambridge were scattered among the colleges which later became the basis of instruction according to a system which still remains in large part intact, in general they did not have the role which we would like to have had them play. Many of them rapidly gained renown: the colleges of Harcourt (1280) and Navarre (1304) with the Sorbonne in Paris; that of Spain established in Bologna in 1307 by Cardinal Albornoz; Balliol (1261–6); Merton (1263–70); University (ca. 1280); Exeter (1314–16); Oriel (1324); Queen's (1341); New College (1379); Lincoln (1429); All Souls, established in 1438 for the repose of the English souls fallen during the Hundred Years War; and Magdalen (1448) in Oxford; Peterhouse (1284); King's Hall; Michaelhouse (1324); University (1326); Pembroke (1347); Gonville (1349); Trinity Hall (1350); Corpus Christi (1352); Godshouse (1441–2); King's College (1441); Queen's College (1448); St Catharine's (1475); and Jesus (1497) in Cambridge. But those establishments, although they naturally attracted schools of thought which did not have buildings of their own, were quite different from the image that has traditionally been given to them. They became the center of a seigneury, rented or bought houses, at first near the towns, then in the countryside and the surrounding villages, and exploited them commercially. They had their jurisdictional rights recognized in the area, regulated traffic in the neighboring streets, lodged large families of magistrates, especially those of the Parlement, in their buildings, notably in Paris. The Sorbonne quarter thus became one of the "judiciary enclaves" of Paris. The colleges were returning to the style of the ancient abbeys. They crystalized the ennoblement of the universities, accentuated their closed character while the university academics and their instruction were increasingly compromised by an oligarchy – primarily of the robe.

Thus the universities themselves became powers anchored in the temporal, landowners whose economic concerns went beyond the administration of corporative affairs, of seigneuries. The seals which had been the insignia of the corporation became the coat of arms of the lady.

THE EVOLUTION OF SCHOLASTICISM

Alongside this social evolution there was a parallel evolution of scholasticism itself which went so far as to reject its fundamental principles. From the extreme complexity of the philosophy and theology of the fourteenth and fifteenth centuries, let us attempt to disengage a few strong currents which flowed away from the scholasticism of the thirteenth century: the critical and skeptical current which originated with Duns Scotus and Ockham; scientific experimentalism which, among the Mertonians at Oxford and the Parisian doctors (Autrecourt, Buridan, and Nicholas Oresme), led to empiricism; Averroism which, as we shall see, beginning with Marsilio of Padua and John of Jandun, ended above all in politics, and which the great heresiarchs Wyclif and Jan Hus came close to adopting. Finally the anti-intellectualism which was soon to color all scholasticism during the decline of the Middle Ages, was fed on the mysticism of Master Eckhart, and was popularized in the fifteenth century by Peter of Ailly, Jean Gerson, and Nicholas of Cusa.

THE DIVORCE BETWEEN REASON AND FAITH

With the help of the great Franciscan doctors John Duns Scotus (1266–1308) and William Ockham (ca. 1300 – ca. 1350), theology attacked the major problem of scholasticism: the balance between reason and faith. After around 1320, as Gorden Leff has pointed out,[2] the Anselmian concept of "faith itself seeking understanding" was abandoned along with the effort to achieve a union between the created and the divine, which had been, through different approaches, the goal of the Augustinians as well as the Thomists. However, the Augustinian school of thought was embraced more in the fourteenth and fifteenth centuries than was Thomism, which, on the contrary, the thinkers of that time were rising up against.

Duns Scotus was the first to attempt to separate reason from the affairs of faith. God was so free that He escaped from human reasoning. As divine freedom was becoming the center of theology, the latter was placed beyond the reach of reason. William Ockham pursued this work and completed the divorce between practical and theoretical knowledge by applying the consequences of Scotist doctrine to man's relationship with God.

[2]   *Past and Present*, April 1956.

PLATE 31 *Nicholas of Cusa*

He distinguished an abstract knowledge from an intuitive knowledge. As opposed to intuitive knowledge, abstract knowledge "does not enable us to know whether a thing which exists, truly exists, or whether a thing which does not exist, does not . . .. Intuitive knowledge is that through which we know that a thing *is*, when it is, and that it is *not*, when it is not." Of course, as Paul Vignaux has shown, Ockhamian logic did not necessarily lead to skepticism. The process of knowledge did not necessarily imply the existence of the known object. Truth was reached through two entirely separate processes: proof dealt only with what one could assure through experience; everything else was a matter of speculation, bringing forth no certainty, and at most only probabilities. But Ockham's own application of these theories to theology ended up in skepticism. God being defined only through his all powerfulness, 'He became synonymous with uncertainty, He was no longer the measure of all things.

Consequently, reason could no longer support or confirm belief. Belief could only abandon the field of discussion, leaving its place to facts, or submit to doubt which ruled over the entire extra-sensible realm."

Michalski has shown well how the Ockhamists, starting with those givens, transformed philosophy and theology into criticism and skepticism. They very teachings of the universities bore the profound mark of this. The commentary of Peter Lombard's *Sentences*, until then the touchstone of theological instruction, was increasingly disdained. After Ockham, *questions* diminished in number and increasingly concentrated on all-powerfulness and free will. The whole balance of nature and grace was simultaneously upset. Man could accomplish all that God asked of him even outside of grace. All dogmatic instruction was worthless. All values became shaken. Good and evil were no longer necessarily exclusive of each other. Human strengths could no longer be discussed except in natural terms, associated with experience.

On the opposite side the adversaries of Ockhamism – such as the Oxfordian Thomas Bradwardine – agreed to place themselves on the same level and posed the same problems. Their authoritarianism, which turned the authority of the dogma into the center of all truth and knowledge, led to an equally radical exclusion of reason. As Gordon Leff has aptly noted, without that destructive work of skeptical theology, "there could have been neither a Renaissance nor a Reform." Henceforth the path was open for a voluntarism which, deformed and perverted, legitimized the will for power, and justified the tyranny of the prince. The last scruples were swept away – such as those of Gabriel Biel, who, defending his master Ockham, asserted that despite everything, he had not betrayed his profession as an intellectual: "It would be shameful for a theologian not to be able to give some knowledge and some reason to believe;" or of Peter of Ailly who declared in very circumspect language: "Our faith is true and, as a consequence, it would be unfitting for it not to be able to be defended and to be sustained with probability."[3]

[3] Leonard A. Kennedy, *Peter of Ailly and the Harvest of XIVth Century Philosophy* (Lewiston, N.Y.: The Edwin Mellen Press, 1986), p. 31. – TRANS.

THE LIMITS OF EXPERIMENTAL SCIENCE

It was that criticism which underlay the logical and scientific work of Mertonians such as William Heybtesbury and Richard Swineshead – heirs, moreover, of Grosseteste and Roger Bacon – and of the Parisians Nicolas d'Autrecourt, Jean Buridan, Albert of Saxony, and Nicholas Oresme. They were satisfied with experience: "I do not propose all that as fact, but I will only ask the gentlemen theologians to explain to me how all of that can happen."

Those masters became the precursors of the great scholars of the beginning of the modern age; Jean Buridan, who was rector of the University of Paris and whom posterity knew paradoxically for his alleged scandalous affair with Joan of Navarre, and for his famous donkey, is believed to have "foreseen the foundations of modern dynamics," having given a definition for the movement of a body which was very close to Galileo's *impeto*, and to Descartes' "quantity of movement." "If someone throws projectiles at an equal speed, a light piece of wood and a heavy piece of iron, those two pieces being moreover of the same volume and the same shape, the piece of iron will go farther because the force which is inherent in it is more intense." Albert of Saxony, with his theory of weight, is thought to have "exercised his influence over the entire development of statics until the middle of the seventeenth century, and led Leonardo da Vinci, Cardano, and Bernard Palissy to the study of fossils." As for Nicholas Oresme, who clearly perceived the law of falling bodies, the diurnal movement of the earth, and the use of coordinates, he was "the direct predecessor of Copernicus." According to Pierre Duhem, his demonstrations were based on arguments whose "clarity and precision far surpass what Copernicus wrote on the same subject." These are debatable views, which have indeed been debated. It remains, however, that even if these scholars had such remarkable intuitions, they remained sterile for a long time. In their search for fertility they came up against bottlenecks of medieval science: the absence of a scientific symbolism capable of translating the principles of their science into clear formulas that could be far-reaching and have

PLATE 32   *The terrestrial sphere, according to Ptolemy (Bibliothèque nationale)*

easy applications; the delay in techniques making it impossible to take advantage of theoretical discoveries; and the tyranny of theology which prevented the "artists" from developing clear scientific ideas. The scholars of the fourteenth century are now beginning to reveal their secrets, thanks to the work of Koyré, Maier, Combes, Clagett, and Beaujouan. But it does seem that they contributed to discrediting rationalism only to wind up at a dead end.

ANTI-INTELLECTUALISM

They were swept up in the entire anti-intellectualist current which henceforth carried thinkers along. The mysticism of Master Eckhart seduced most of the intellectuals at the end of the Middle Ages. In 1449 Cardinal Nicholas of Cusa, the author of the last great scholastic *summa* of the Middle Ages, came to Eckhart's defense, attacked Aristotelianism, and wrote the *Apology of Learned Ignorance*:

> The greatest danger against which the sages have warned us, is that which results from the communication of what is secret to minds enslaved by the authority of an inveterate habit, for so powerful is a long observance of authorities that most people prefer to give up life rather than their habits; we can see this regarding the persecutions inflicted on the Jews, the Saracens, and on other hardened heretics, who affirm their opinion as law, confirmed by the usage of time, which they place above their own lives. Now today it is the Aristotelian sect which prevails and it considers as a heresy the coincidence of the opposite ideas the admission of which alone enables an ascent toward mystical theology. To those who have been nourished in that sect, that path appears absolutely insipid and contrary to their purpose. This is why they quickly reject it and it would be a true miracle, a true religious conversion, if, in rejecting Aristotle, they progressed toward new heights.

And after coming to Eckhart's defense he concludes with this statement:

I deliver these declarations to you so that you will read them and, if you deem necessary, have others read them, so that through your internal warmth this admirable sowing will grow and we will rise toward the vision of divine realities. For I have already heard that thanks to your fervent efforts this sowing communicated through Italy to zealous minds will bear much fruit. There is absolutely no doubt that this speculation will triumph over all the philosophers' means of rationalizing even though it is difficult to renounce accepted usages. And insofar as you will progress, do not forget to keep me constantly informed of your progress. For it is only there that in a sort of divine pasture I joyfully regain my strength, insofar as God allows me, using Learned Ignorance and endlessly aspiring to take pleasure in that life which for the moment I perceive only through distant images, but toward which I attempt each day to get a little closer. May God, so desired and forever blessed, grant us, delivered from this world, to finally reach it. Amen.[4]

Already in the middle of the fourteenth century Richard Fitzralph had given as an example his own conversion from philosophy to a fideistic theology expressed in a prayer to Christ to whom he declared: "Until I had you, you who are the Truth, to guide me, I had heard, without understanding, the tumult of the philosophers whose ramblings were directed against you, the astute Jews, superb Greeks, materialist Saracens, ignorant Armenians . . ." And in his *summa* he deliberately abandons scholastic arguments and uses only texts from the Bible.

Henceforth the great enemy, as we have already seen in Nicholas of Cusa, was Aristotle. "Earlier," Fitzralph continues, "my thought was attached to the teachings of Aristotle and to arguments which appeared profound only to men who were profoundly vain." Peter of Ailly, who was rector of Paris, echoed him: "There are no, or few, evidently demonstrative arguments in philosophy or in the teaching of Aristotle. Also, it follows that the philosophy or teaching of Aristotle ought rather to be called

---

[4]   Translated into English from the French version by de Gandillac.

PLATE 33   *Gerson portrayed as a pilgrim (Bibliothèque nationale)*

opinion than knowledge. And therefore those who cling too tenaciously to the authority of Aristotle are very reprehensible."[5]

Such also was the thought of Jean Gerson, that other illustrious chancellor of the University of Paris at the turn of the fourteenth and fifteenth centuries. Some scholars have attributed to him *The Imitation of Christ*, which declares:

[5]   Kennedy, *Peter of Ailly*, p. 35. – TRANS.

Many weary and strain themselves to acquire knowledge, and I have seen, said the Sage, that that, too, is vanity and the vexation of the spirit. What good will it be to you to know things of this world when this world itself will have passed? On the last day you will not be asked what you have learned, but what you have done, and there will be no more learning in Hell, toward which you are rushing. Cease your vain labor.

Thus scholasticism ceded its place to a return of holy ignorance, rational knowledge bowed its head before an affective piety of which the pious sermons and opuscules of Gerson and Ailly were the expression. Thus academics approached a certain humanist spirituality, that of the *devotio moderna*, and we know the seductive influence it exercised over Erasmus.

THE NATIONALIZATION OF UNIVERSITIES: THE NEW UNIVERSITY GEOGRAPHY

In the course of these two centuries the universities also lost their international character. The principal cause of this was the establishment of many new universities whose recruitment became increasingly national or even regional.

In the thirteenth century the progress of the Spanish Reconquista and the strengthening of the authority of the Iberian monarchs gave birth in the peninsula to establishments which, although some of them developed schools which were already in existence, no longer had that character of spontaneous and progressive formation found in Bologna, Paris, and Oxford. They were most often veritable creations in which kings and popes collaborated.

Following the failure to establish a university in Palencia, the University of Salamanca was born between 1220 and 1230 thanks to the efforts of Alfonso IX of Laon. It was definitively established in 1254 with the charter of Alfonso X the Wise, himself an illustrious scholar, and with the confirmation bull of Pope Alexander IV in 1255. There was then the successive appearance of universities in Lisbon and Coimbra (1290),

Lerida (1300), Perpignan (1350), Huesca (1354), Barcelona (1450), Saragossa (1470), Palma of Majorca (1483), Siguenza (1489), Alcala (1499), and Valencia (1500).

Beginning in the fourteenth century the countries of central, eastern, and northern Europe were caught up in the movement. The first university in the Holy Roman Empire, Prague was created in 1347 by Pope Clement VI upon the request of Charles IV, who primarily wanted to favor his kingdom of Bohemia with a university. There then came the universities of Vienna, founded by Rudolf IV and Urban V in 1365, and reestablished by Albert III in 1383; Erfurt, which, armed with the bulls of two popes (Clement VII in 1379 and Urban VI in 1384) emerged only, however, in 1392; Heidelberg (1385); Cologne (1388); Leipzig, which emerged in 1409 from crises in Prague; Rostock (1419); Trier, which, although founded in 1454, only truly existed after 1473; Greifswald (1456); Freiburg-im-Breisgau (1455–6); Basel (1459); Ingolstadt, which after obtaining a bull

PLATE 34   *Faculty of Theology in Salamanca. Fray Luis de Leon preached from this pulpit.*

from Pius II in 1459 was organized only in 1472; Mainz (1476); and Tübingen (1476–7). However, the University of Louvain, founded in 1425, attracted students from Burgundian countries. Cracow, founded by Casimir the Great in 1364, was established by Ladislaus Jagello with the help of Boniface IX in 1397–1400; Pecs taught canon law starting in 1367; Budapest, founded in 1389 flourished temporarily in 1410; and Pressburg was founded in 1465–7. Sweden had its university in Upsala in 1477; Denmark had its own in Copenhagen in 1478. Whereas Oxford and Cambridge cornered the market in the English scholarly world, the Scottish kings founded three universities: St Andrews (1413), Glasgow (1450–1), and Aberdeen (1494).

In Italy short-lived universities, created often by masters and students fleeing from Bologna or elsewhere, were formed in Modena, Reggio Emilia, Vicenza, Arezzo, Vercelli, Siena, and Treviso. Naples, founded by Frederick II as a war machine against the papacy, had brilliant moments only under the reign of that king. Other universities were important only through the support of Italian princes who wanted to make them a central part of their states. The primary one was in Padua, founded in 1222, which beginning in 1404 became the university of the

PLATE 35   *Seal of the University of Cambridge (Bibliothèque nationale)*

Venetian republic. In 1244 Innocent IV established a university near the pontifical court which the popes attempted to vivify in the fourteenth and fifteenth centuries as they strengthened their authority within the Church. Siena, which had its own university as of 1246, reestablished it in 1357 with a bull of the Emperor Charles IV, and again in 1408 with new privileges from Pope Gregory XII. The University of Piacenza, nominally founded in 1248, was brought back to life by Gian Galeazzo Visconti in 1398 to become the intellectual center of the Milanese state, a role it abandoned in 1412 to Pavia, which had been founded in 1361. Between 1349 and 1472 Florence played an important role as the premier humanist center, but at that time Lorenzo the Magnificent preferred Pisa, which had existed since 1343 as a university seat for the Florentine state. In 1430 the Estes brought back a university which had been founded in 1391 in Ferrara. Beginning in 1405 the Piedmont duchy had a university in Turin which experienced vicissitudes, and Alfonso the Magnificent, king of Aragon and Sicily, founded a university in Catania in 1444 with the help of Pope Eugenius IV.

The final example of attempts at university regionalization was that of France. Besides the universities of Paris, Montpellier, and Orleans, born out of scholarly centers which in the twelfth century were already quite considerable, and besides Angers, whose history is obscure, Toulouse was, as we know, founded in 1229 to fight against the Albigensian heresy. Other foundations, due in large part to military events, brought about only short-lived or obscure universities. Avignon, founded by Boniface VIII in 1303, was prosperous only during the stay of the popes. Cahors, founded in 1332, lasted only a short time; Grenoble, founded by Humbert II, stagnated after 1339; imperial Orange had hardly any greater success between 1365 and 1475. After 1409 Louis II of Provence attracted Burgundians, Provençals, and Catalonians to Aix, according to the terminology of the nations at Montpellier. The university of Dôle, founded by Philip the Good, duke of Burgundy, with the help of Pope Martin V, disappeared in 1481. Valence owed to the Dauphin, the future Louis XI, a university which was active only in law after 1452. As king he founded a university in his hometown of

Bourges in 1464, whereas the duke of Brittany created one in Nantes in 1460, which was revived by Charles VIII in 1498.

The division of France between the English and Charles VII gave birth to three universities which ultimately prospered: Caen (1432) and Bordeaux (1441) on the English side, and Poitiers (1431) on the French side. Setting Montpellier aside due to its medical speciality, Paris remained the great intellectual center of France or of those in the French orbit.

However, this increase in the number of universities was enough to reduce, if not to completely halt, international recruitment by the most important universities, and in any event to ruin the system of nations, so important until then since this system was very often a central part of the university structure. Pearl Kibre has traced the disappearance of university nations throughout the fourteenth and fifteenth centuries.[6]

ACADEMICS AND POLITICS

This process occurred in a general evolution which saw the large universities at the end of the Middle Ages become political powers, play an active role, sometimes in the forefront, in struggles between states; become theaters of violent crises where the "nations" within their folds, henceforth inspired by national feeling, came into conflict; and in the end become integrated into the new national structures of the states. We can briefly trace this evolution through the political Averroism of Ockham and Marsilio of Padua, the crises of the University of Prague, and the political role of the University of Paris.

George de Lagarde, in a famous series of studies on the birth of the lay spirit at the end of the Middle Ages, has minutely analyzed the theses and political activities of William of Ockham and Marsilio of Padua. Despite the differences which separated the two men in the first half of the fourteenth century, alongside Emperor Louis IV of Bavaria they both waged a common battle against the papacy and its temporal pretentions.

---

[6]   See *The Nations in the Medieval Universities*, 1948.

Out of their work as polemicists and political theorists there emerged the masterpiece of Marsilio of Padua, the *Defensor Pacis.* It is easy to note the traditions which inspired its writing, beyond the spirit of the Italian communes. First there was the Ghibelline tradition which opposed pontifical aspirations to temporal domination and supported both the principle of the separation of spiritual and temporal powers, and the Emperor's claim to the latter. Philosophically they were inspired by an Averroist tradition which interpreted Aristotle quite differently than Thomism did, and which resulted, in the realm of social philosophy, in an empiricism defined rather badly by the term "naturalism" insofar as it tends "to liberate politics from morality," to give preference to individual will over profound objective realities, to reduce the social *order* to a mechanical balance of powers, and to substitute *convention* for *nature.* In

PLATE 36   *Christ giving the pope and the emperor the symbols of spiritual authority and temporal power*

addition there was the influence of the legists and the Dubois/ Nogaret clan who, with Philip the Fair, at the turn of the thirteenth and fourteenth centuries, had already waged a pitiless battle against the papacy in defense of the emerging monarchy.

The conclusion was the *complete* state, the affirmation of the autonomy of the state, based on the separation of law and morality. The positivist conception of social life led to the divine right of the established order. "If you resist secular authority, even if its holders are infidels or perverse, you will risk eternal damnation." The all-powerful state claimed all rights in the social realm, rights whose unity was strongly proclaimed; it had legislative, executive, and juridical power. It was universal: on a given territory no subject could escape the authority of the prince. In the end the secular state was not content simply to relegate the Church to the spiritual realm; it claimed a spiritual mission for itself, the right also to rule in that realm. It ultimately dissolved all true distinction between the spiritual and the temporal:

> Surely it is not for a human legislator . . . to create or to halt spiritual precepts, they being nothing other than injunctions or permissions from God Himself. But it is for the human legislator or judge to know of all the licit or illicit acts carried out or omitted by men, lay or priests, ministers or secular, both in spiritual matters as well as temporal ones, under the condition, however, that it does not concern a strictly spiritual matter.

One can almost hear Luther speaking: "All that is not the life of intimate grace, all that materializes the life of the Church is of the world, and belongs to the State. All that is execution of moral law in the age escapes the Church and falls to the State."

This was an explosive doctrine which would continue and appear in philosophies as different as those of Machiavelli or Luther, of Hobbes or Rousseau, of Hegel or Auguste Compte, of Lenin or Charles Maurras.

But what distinguished Ockham and especially Marsilio of Padua from the Ghibelline tradition is that they no longer ultimately dreamt of uniting into a single imperial lay state, if not all of humanity, at least all of western Christian Europe.

There is a fundamental difference – and here especially – between Marsilio of Padua and Dante, for whom the emperor should have been, on the contrary, the restorer of basic unity. Scholastic polity sought to extend to all men the city of Aristotle transformed into a Christian city. Marsilian polity admitted the diversity of nations and states. As one reads in the *Defensor Pacis*:

> As to whether it is advantageous to have one supreme government in number for all those who live a civil life in the whole world, or whether on the contrary it is at a certain time advantageous to have different such governments in different regions of the world which are almost necessarily separate from one another in place, and especially for men who use different languages and who differ widely in morals and customs . . . . The heavenly cause moves perhaps toward the latter alternative, in order that the procreation of men may not become excessive. For one might perhaps think that nature, by means of wars and epidemics, has moderated the procreation of men and other animals.[7]

Political Ockhamism and Averroism – if they supported an extreme thesis, one quite beyond the conditions of the fourteenth century, but which had considerable repercussions – agreed with a general tendency of intellectual reflection applied to the examination of political evolution. The tendency was to accept the end of unity, here as well, to submit to division, to join the side that was breaking Christendom apart. The tendency was toward particularism.

THE FIRST NATIONAL UNIVERSITY: PRAGUE

There was even a tendency toward national sentiment, as is seen in the example of Prague. The university was founded there in the midst of turmoil. As international as all other universities, it

---

[7] *Marsilius of Padua: The Defender of Peace.* Vol. II: *The Defensor Pacis*, translated with an introduction by Alan Gewirth (New York: Columbia University Press, 1956), pp. 84–85. – Trans.

PLATE 37 *Dante (artist anonymous) Courtesy Alinari-Giraudon)*

was soon threatened with being taken over by the German masters and students who were all the more numerous since they had fled from Paris at the time of the Great Schism. They clashed with the Czech contingent, which had become increasingly conscious of its originality and aspirations. This ethnic opposition was doubled by a corporative opposition: there was a question of knowing whether the *nations* dominated by the Germans would win out over the Czech *nation*, and what would be the distribution of chairs and university positions among the different groups. All of this was based on a social opposition: the Czechs were associated with the popular classes – native peasants and artisans – whereas the Germans who had settled in the country represented primarily the bourgeois wealth of the cities, the nobility and the clergy.

It took a figure of class, Jan Hus, who with the help of his friends brought a philosophical and theological doctrine which

PLATE 38 *Jan Hus (Bibliothèque nationale)*

owed much to Oxford and Wyclif, who was able to connect the university milieu and the popular milieux of Prague and Bohemia, who inspired his listeners through his eloquence and his passion, and who exercised enough pressure on the stupid king of Bohemia, Wenceslaus IV, for the conflict to erupt and be resolved in favor of the Czechs by the royal decree of Kutna Hora in 1409. While most of the *nations* were overthrown to the benefit of the Czechs, all members of the university had henceforth to swear an oath of allegiance to the crown of Bohemia. The Germans left the University of Prague and went to found that of Leipzig. This was an important date in medieval history: a national university was born; the intellectual world was sliding into political molds.

But the path which had led the University of Paris to be integrated into the national monarchy was beset with obstacles.

PARIS: THE GRANDEUR AND WEAKNESS OF UNIVERSITY POLITICS

With the flight of many English during the Hundred Years War, and of many Germans at the time of the Great Schism, the University of Paris was already tending to become primarily French in its recruitment. Since at least the reign of Philip the Fair it played a political role of primary importance. Charles V called it "the eldest daughter of the king." It was officially represented in the national councils of the Church of France and in the assemblies of the States General. Its intervention was requested at the time of the fight between Etienne Marcel and other Parisians and the Royal Court; at the time of the Maillotin uprising; and it was a signatory to the Treaty of Troyes.

The university's prestige was enormous. It was not derived simply from its effective student or instructor members, but from all the former masters who throughout France and abroad occupied positions of primary importance and had maintained close ties with the university.

However, it remained attached to the papacy, all the more since the popes of Avignon, all French, favored it considerably. They associated themselves with the university through bonds of ever greater largesse. Thus there was each year a list sent to the court of Avignon, a *rotulus nominandorum*, containing the names of masters for whom the university was asking the pope to give special provisions or expectative favors of ecclesiastical benefices. If the university was "the eldest daughter of the king of France," it was also "the first school of the Church," and played an international role as arbiter in theological matters.

The Schism upset that balance. At first the university opted for the pope of Avignon, then, tired of the growing demands of the papacy and concerned with reestablishing the unity of the Church, it induced the king of France to repudiate, momentarily, the Avignon papacy and relentlessly demanded the convocation of a council to put an end to the Schism with the abdication of the rival pontiffs. At the same time the university made itself the champion of the council's superiority over the pope, and of the relative independence of the national Church with regard to the Holy See, it made itself the champion of Gallicanism. But if the first stance won the university great prestige within the Christian world, the second one tended to detach it from the papacy only to place it under the growing influence of the monarchy.

Its success finally seemed to be affirmed. The council of Constance, where it played a leading role, seemed to confirm its triumph. One notes, however, some curious attitudes of certain academics. As E. F. Jacob has shown,[8] the English academics, against all expectations, took the side of the papacy in the collation of benefices. They were thinking of their own interests, which were better served by the papacy.

But the council of Basel, where academics played only a small role, ended in failure and the victory of the papacy. In the meantime a serious crisis, this time French, had greatly shaken the position of the University of Paris.

Troubles in the reign of Charles VI ended with the Caboche-inspired uprising in Paris, and with the dividing of the country between the English and the French, Paris being the capital of the English king. Undoubtedly the university did not immediately, nor entirely, embrace the Burgundian party. The duke relied on the mendicant orders to which the university was traditionally opposed. It had condemned the work of Jean Petit, the apologist of the murder of the Duke of Orleans. At the time of the English conquest many masters left Paris, surrounded the Dauphin, formed the administrative framework of the kingdom of Bourges, and eventually established the new University of Poitiers.

But those who had remained in Paris, after turning into Burgundians, submitted themselves to the English will. The most famous episode of this "English" period in the University of Paris was the action the university took against Joan of Arc. By showing its hostility toward her – despite Gerson – it succeeded only in pleasing its foreign master. It was also following popular opinion, which was very hostile to the Maid of Orleans, as is

---

[8] Bulletin of the John Rylands Library, 1946.

shown in the *Bourgeois de Paris,* among other writings. It also showed the degree to which its intellectuals, so full of themselves, were incapable of parting with their arrogance as scholars in the face of the glorious naivety, the candid ignorance of Joan. We know that the university conducted the trial against the Maid, and announced her condemnation to the king of England with unhidden satisfaction.

The ashes at the stake in Rouen had soiled the prestige of the university. Also, once Paris was recaptured, Charles VII, and then Louis XI, demonstrated their distrust of the "collaborator" who however supported their Gallican politics and vigorously upheld the pragmatic sanction.

In 1437 the king took away the university's fiscal privileges and forced it to contribute to the "aids" levied for the recon-quering of Montereau. In 1445 its judiciary privilege was in turn revoked and it became subject to the Parlement. The king supported the reorganization undertaken in 1452 by Cardinal d'Estouteville, the pontifical legate. In 1470 Louis XI ordered all masters and students who were Burgundian subjects to swear an oath of obedience to him. Finally in 1499 the university lost its right to strike. It was in the hands of the king.

During all these struggles, what became of the spirit of teaching? It underwent a dual evolution, and this enables us to better understand the relationship between scholasticism and humanism, to provide nuance to their opposition, and to per-ceive the passage from the one to the other in that passing of the intellectual torch.

THE SCLEROSIS OF SCHOLASTICISM

On the one hand, scholasticism was becoming weak, despite interesting efforts of renovation, despite the work of Nicholas of Cusa, who was interested in reconciling tradition with new needs. It continued, moreover, to tear itself apart. On the one hand, there were the *ancients,* who were then the Aristotelians and the Thomists, and who were winded quibblers. On the other hand, there were the *moderns* who gathered under the banner of

PLATE 40   *The Theologian (illustration by Holbein for* The Praise of Folly
by Erasmus) (Bibliotèque nationale)

Ockhamian nominalism. But they were shut up in the study of
formal logic, in endless lucubrations about the definition of
words, in artificial divisions and subdivisions, in *terminism*. In
1474 Louis XI banned the *ancients'* teaching and books by an
edict revoked in 1481. The most active were perhaps the Scotists,
who attempted in vain to reconcile an increasingly verbal
criticism with an increasingly cloudy fideist voluntarism. They
were the favorite victims of the attacks of Erasmus and Rabelais,
who heaped their irony or sarcasm upon the *Scotists*, prototypes
of the scholastics. Rabelais, moreover, put them all in the same
boat in the burlesque catalog which the young Pantagruel leafs
through in the library of St Victor. Soon Thomas Bricot, "a very
ingenious interpreter of the nominalists," Pierre Tateret, the
head of Parisian Scotism after 1490, Pierre Crockart, a renovator

of the teaching of Thomism, Noël Bédier, John Major, and Jacques Almain, all notorious Ockhamists, were offered up as fodder for mockery.

It was this verbalism that was also mocked by Villon, whose distracted ear, better than anyone else's, heard only the hollow sounds of words in the lectures at the Sorbonne:

> Finally, being here alone
>> To-night and in good trim to write,
> I heard the clocks of the Sorbonne,
>> That aye at nine o'clock of night
>> Is wont the Angelus to smite:
> Then I my task did intermit,
>> That to our Lady mild I might
> Do suit and service, as is fit.
>
> This done, I half forgot myself,
>> What while I felt Dame Memory
> Take in and lay upon her shelf
>> (The wit, as 'twere, being bound in me,
>> Though not for wine-bibbing, perdie,)
> Her faculties collateral,
>> Th' opinative in each degree
> And others intellectual.
>
> And on likewise th' estimative,
>> – whereby prosperity we gain, –
> Similative and formative,
>> By whose disorder folk remain
>> Oft lunatic, to wit, insane,
> From month to month; which aforesaid
>> I mind me often and again
> In Aristotle to have read.[9]

It was this depraved, caricatured, moribund scholasticism that the humanists above all rejected.

[9] From Villon's "The Lesser Testament," translated by John Payne, in *The Complete Poems of François Villon/The Testaments of François Villon*, translated by John Heron Lepper, including the texts of John Payne and others (New York: Liveright Publishing Corp., 1924), p. 191. – TRANS.

ACADEMICS   OPEN   UP   TO   HUMANISM

However, university instruction was opening up in another way to these new tastes. First in the Italian universities, where scholasticism did not have the same traditions as in Paris or Oxford, where the tradition of ancient letters had been better maintained and was awakened earlier with the Roman renewal, and where the ebbing of Byzantine science in the face of the Turkish threat supported the resurgence of Hellenism. In Bologna Pietro di Muglio taught rhetoric from 1371 to 1382, but Coluccio Salutati did without it. Greek had been taught there since 1424 and Filelfo was able to win part of some initially indifferent students over to it. Above all, between 1450 and 1455 the famous cardinal Bessarion reorganized the university for the pope in his capacity as rector and as governor of the city. The teaching of the *humanities* (*studia humanitatis*) in Bologna was never to cease.

Padua was perhaps even more precocious and in the fifteenth century its annexation by Venice brilliantly encouraged the study of Greek there, at which Aldus Manutius marvelled. Following Guarino, Filelfo, Vittorino da Feltre, the Byzantine refugees continued the tradition with Demetrius Chalcondyles and Marc Mousourous. Here, even more than in Bologna, Bessarion's influence was profound.

The emerging seigneuries favored these currents. In Florence, in addition to the famous Platonic Academy, the university, with Ambrose of Camaldoli, Aurispa, Guarino, and Filelfo, studied Cicero and Terence, Lucian, Pindar, Demosthenes, Plotinus, Proclus, Philo, and Strabo. When Lorenzo the Magnificent moved the University of Florence to Pisa in 1472, chairs in poetry, eloquence, mathematics, and astronomy were immediately established. The Visconti, then the Sforza, who had very close relationships with France, did the same in Pavia in the fifteenth century and during the Italian wars. In Ferrara the Estes followed these policies and called upon one of the principal Hellenists of the time, Theodore Gaza, to be professor and rector. At the Sapienza at Rome, there was the same fervor for classical letters taught by Filelfo, Enoc d'Ascoli, Argyropulos, and Theodore Gaza.

But neither Oxford nor Paris were impermeable to humanism, nor was Prague where a refined humanist circle, open to Italian influences – from Petrarch to Cola di Rienzo – was formed in the middle of the fourteenth century alongside Charles IV and the new university. Already at the beginning of the fourteenth century Nicholas Trivet, who had taught at Oxford, London, and Paris, was making commentaries on the declamations of Seneca the Elder, the tragedies of Seneca the Younger, and Titus-Livius. Above all, the gift of Duke Humphrey of Gloucester to the University of Oxford in 1439 and 1443 of his library rich in Greek and Latin classics and in works by the Italians, disseminated the spirit of humanism there. Oxford was ready for the lessons of Linacre, Grocyn, Colet, and Thomas More. It was waiting for Erasmus.

PLATE 41   *Thomas More with his family (drawing by Holbein) Courtesy Roger Viollet)*

The first generation of French humanists with Jean de Montreuil, Nicholas of Clémanges, Gontier Col, and William Fillastre, had ties with the University of Paris. It was for his being a humanist that Jean de Montreuil praised the chancellor Gerson in a letter to William Fillastre:

> Whereas according to rumor nothing of what one can know escapes you, and I know many signs of this, I do not cease to be amazed that you do not follow in the footsteps of the illustrious chancellor of Paris, an exceptionally cultivated man. I am not speaking of his life nor his manners, nor even of his knowledge of the Christian religion or of theoretical theology, in which you have both achieved such distinction and greatness. I am speaking of the art of speaking and persuasion which rests above all on the rules of rhetoric and eloquence thanks to which one achieves it and without which expression, which seems to me to be the goal of culture, is reduced to being ineffectual, empty, and hollow.

The theologian Guillaume Fichet, a friend of Bessarion, who in 1470 introduced the printing press to the Collège de Sorbonne, sought to reconcile his admiration for Petrarch with his respect for the Thomist tradition, and hoped for the resurrection of Platonism. Robert Gaguin, dean of the faculty of canon law, grouped humanists who were enthusiasts of Petrarch around him, and was in close rapport with the Florentines. If Erasmus, disgusted by the barbarous discipline which Jan Standonck caused to reign at Montaigu College, conceived during his stay at the university only scorn for the decadent scholasticism which was being taught there, Jacques Lefevre of Etaples, master of arts, professor at the college of Cardinal Lemoine, spread one of the purest forms of humanism in Paris, concerning which one should reread the beautiful pages of Augustin Renaudet.

It remains that, even if humanism attacked particularly a petrified scholasticism, and if academics sometimes allowed themselves to be drawn into humanism, there was a profound difference between the medieval intellectual and the humanist of the Renaissance.

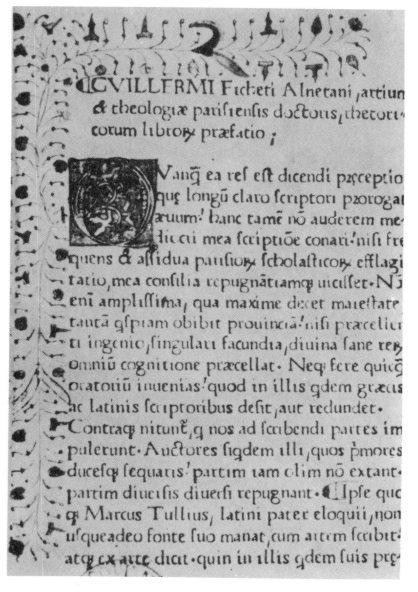

GVILLERMI Ficheti Alnetani, artiun
& theologiæ parifienfis doctoris, thetori-
corum libroჳ præfatio ;

Vanჟ ea ref eft dicendi pჳceptio
ჟuჳ longŭ claro fcriptori pჳorogat
æuum! hanc tamē nō auderem me-
dicci mea fcriptiōe conati-'nifi fre
quens & affidua parifioჳ fcholafticoჳ efflagi
ratio, mea confilia repugnātiamჟ incidfet· Nჳ
enī ampliffima, qua maxime decet maieftate
tautā qfpiam obibit prouincia-'nifi præcelici
ti ingenio, fingulari facundia, diuina fane reჳ
omniŭ cognitione præcellat· Neჟ fere quicჟ
oratoriŭ inuenias-'quod in illis qdem græcis
ac latinis fcriptoribus defit, aut redundet·
Contracჟ nitunຮ, q nos ad fcribendi partes im
puletunt· Auctores fiqdem illi, quos þmores
ducefჟ fequaris' partim iam olim nō extant·
partim diuerfis diuerfi repugnant· Ipfe quc
ჟ Marcus Tullius, latini pater eloquii, non
ufqueadeo fonte fuo manat, cum artem fcribit·
atჟ ex arte dicit·quin in illis qdem fuis pჳ

PLATE 42 *First book printed at the Sorbonne (Bibliothèque nationale)*

THE RETURN TO POETRY AND MYSTICISM

The humanist was profoundly anti-intellectual. He was more literary than scientific, more fideist than rationalist. To the dialectics/scholasticism duo he contrasted the philology/rhetoric duo. With him Plato, discredited as a philosopher by Albert the Great, due to his language and his style, returned to grace, and because he was a poet, was considered to be the "Supreme Philosopher."

Lefevre of Etaples, although he provided an admirable edition of Aristotle's *Nichomachean Ethics*, leaned more toward poets and mystics. His ideal was contemplative knowledge. He published the *Hermetical Books* – in Marsilio Ficino's translation – the works of Pseudo-Denis, the contemplations of the Franciscan Raymond Lull, the mystics Richard of St-Victor, St Hildegard of Bingen, Ruysbroeck, and Nicholas of Cusa, who had made himself the apostle of *Learned Ignorance*.

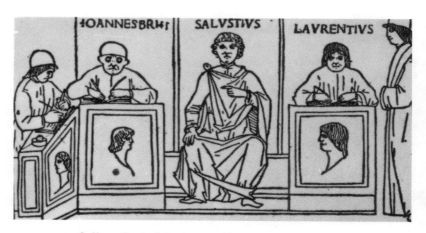

PLATE 43   *Sallust flanked by his two Italian translators, Lorenzo Valla and Giovanni Bri (Bibliothèque nationale)*

Lorenzo Valla himself, that rigorous philologist, the strictest humanist of the quattrocento, preaching in the church of the Dominicans of Rome on March 7, 1457 in honor of St Thomas Aquinas, declared his distaste for Aquinas' method:

> Many are convinced that one cannot become a theologian without knowing the precepts of dialectics, metaphysics, and of all philosophy. What can one say? Would I fear saying all that I think? I praise the extreme subtlety of St Thomas's expression, I admire his diligence, I am amazed in the presence of the richness, the variety, and the perfection of his doctrine . . . .. But I do not so much admire the so-called metaphysics, cumbersome knowledge that is better ignored, because they prevent knowing better things.

True theology for him – as for Lefevre of Etaples – was in St Paul, who does not speak "as an empty and deceptive philosopher" (*per philosophiam et inanem fallaciam*).

Philosophy had to be veiled in the folds of rhetoric and poetry. Its perfect form was the Platonic dialogue.

In the first half of the fifteenth century a revealing controversy had opposed a scholastic and a humanist over the translation of Aristotle.

CONCERNING ARISTOTLE: THE RETURN TO BEAUTIFUL LANGUAGE

In Florence Leonardo Bruni had published a new translation of Aristotle's *Nichomachean Ethics*. This work was indispensable, he said, since the earlier translator, Robert Grosseteste, and not William of Moerbeke, as was believed, working for St Thomas, had little knowledge either of Greek or Latin, committed errors, and wrote in barbarous language.

Cardinal Alonso Garcia of Cartagene, bishop of Burgos and professor at the University of Salamanca, replied to him in no uncertain terms.

PLATE 44   *Miniature illustrating Nicholas Oresme's translation of
Aristotle's* Ethics *(Courtesy Giraudon)*

The debate, he saw clearly, was between form and substance.
For the humanists the former was everything, for scholastics it
was only the servant of thought.

"My response," said Alonso Garcia, "is that Leonardo, if he
has shown enough eloquence, has shown proof of very little
philosophic culture." He revealed the betrayals to Aristotelian
thought committed by the humanist in search of beautiful turns
of phrase, and comes to the defense of the earlier translator,
whose intention he explains:

He has not only translated Aristotle's books from Greek into
Latin, but he has interpreted him with as much truth as possible,
and neither the greatest elegance nor the most beautiful ornaments would have failed him if he had wanted to use them . . ..
But the earlier translator, who adhered more to philosophical
truth, did not want an excess of ornamentation so as to avoid the
errors into which the latter one has fallen. Indeed, he saw clearly
that the Latin tongue could not aspire to the same richness of
expression as does Greek.

And to give the humanist a lesson in historical philology:

> The Latin tongue has not ceased to borrow not only from the Greeks but from barbarous peoples and from all peoples on earth. Likewise, Latin was later enriched by Gallic and Germanic words. Is it not better when there is a popular equivalent which is short and exact to use it rather than resort to long circumlocutions in a classical language?

One heard the same response on the part of the scholastic John Major, who was irritated by the mockeries of the 'Erasmians' and the "Fabrists" against the barbarism of the old style: "Science has no need of beautiful language."

Undoubtedly scholastic Latin was dying out and no longer expressed anything but a science which was itself a fossil. The vernacular tongues to which the future belonged were gaining ground and there were the humanists to help them do so. But humanist Latin definitively turned Latin into a dead language. It took from science the only international language it could have beyond numbers and formulas. It turned it into the antiquated treasure of an elite.

THE ARISTOCRATIC HUMANIST

For the humanist was an aristocrat. If the intellectual of the Middle Ages ultimately betrayed his vocation of *working* scientifically, he did so by denying his own nature. From the start the humanist took the mind, genius, as his symbol, even when he grew pale poring over texts or when his eloquence smelled of the lamp. He wrote for the members of the club. When Erasmus published the *Adagia* his friends told him "You are revealing our mysteries!"

Indeed, the environment in which the humanist was born was quite different from the feverish urban workplace, open to all, one concerned with making progress on all fronts in all forms of technology, and with having them tie into a common economy – the environment where the medieval intellectual had been formed.

The humanist's milieu was that of the group, of the closed *Academy* and, when true humanism conquered Paris, it was not taught at the university, but in that elite institution, the Collège des Lecteurs Royaux, the future Collège de France.

His milieu was the prince's court. At the very heart of the philological quarrel which set him against Leonardo Bruni, Alonso Garcia seemed to have had a premonition of that:

> "Urbanity" denotes for you that "humanity" which as much through words as through gestures goes before honors. One denotes by the name of "urbane" those who have assumed the habit of bending their knees, of lowering their hood, of refusing precedence and first place even among equals. But we call those people "curial," or if that word displeases you since it has another meaning in civil law, and if you permit me to use the vulgar tongue, we call them "courtiers," and their "urbanity" we call "curialism," or, to use a word from courtly language, we call it "courtesy."

Baldassare Castiglione, less than a century later, summed up the social ideal of the humanists in *Il Cortegiano* – "The Courtier."

Here etymology assumes all its significance. From the world of the city (*urbs*) we have gone to the world of the court. Intellectually different, the humanists were even further removed socially from the medieval intellectuals.

From the start their milieu was the protection of the powerful, the bureaucracy, material wealth. Gontier Col was the recipient of "aids" in France and in Normandy (where he trafficked with Charles of Navarre), the secretary to the duke of Berry, the notary and later the secretary of the king, the overseer of the finances of the aids, and one of the king's two treasurers, charged with missions and embassies. Hated by the people, his private home in Paris was pillaged by Caboche's followers. Already the son of rich bourgeois parents, which enabled him to prolong his studies, he profited from his benefactors and from his offices and considerably increased his fortune. Ennobled, he had the control of several houses in Sens, the seigneury of Paron with a vineyard, and a private house in Paris, on rue Vieille-du-Temple. He led a lavish lifestyle, employed many servants, had tapestries, horses, dogs, falcons, and was very fond of gambling. All of that did not prevent him from praising, like the ancients, *sancta simplicitas*. He was a member of Charles VI's *Cour Amoureuse*, presided over by the dukes of Burgundy and Bourbon.

Jean de Montreuil accumulated protectors and duties; he was secretary to the king, to the Dauphin, to the dukes of Berry, Burgundy, and Orleans, and liked to flaunt his influence among his aquaintances ("You who prefer," they told him with flattery, "to use your credit at court for your friends rather than yourself"). At the same time he accumulated ecclesiastical prebends. If he remained a bachelor it was out of pure egoism:

> You have spoiled us, Lord hallelujah!
> You have delivered us from the yoke of marriage, hallelujah!

In a letter to Cardinal Amedee of Saluzzo he claimed to be "filled to satiety." He had "a mountain of books, supplies for a year, several lodgings, clothes, horses, art objects to the point of excess. He [was] a bachelor, he [had] incomparable friends"; concerning which he schemed to obtain a fat benefice.

The prince reserved civil matters for himself. The humanists served him often, but always left the guidance of society to him. They worked in silence. Moreover, they hid the fact that they worked. They praised leisure, free time spent with *belles-lettres*, the *otium* of ancient aristocracy. "Do not be ashamed of this illustrious and glorious leisure in which great minds have always taken pleasure," wrote Nicholas of Clémanges to Jean de Montreuil.

THE RETURN TO THE COUNTRYSIDE

Where better to find that distinguished and studious leisure than in the country? The movement which took the intellectual from the cities and returned him to the country was now complete. Here, too, the agreement between economic and social evolution became perfect. The wealthy bourgeois and princes invested their capital in land, had villas or palaces built, either modest or

luxurious depending on their means. The neo-Platonic Academy
of Florence met in the Medicis' villa at Careggi.

Jean de Montreuil, Nicholas of Clémanges, and Gontier Col
all owned villas where they went for humanist leisure. Jean de
Montreuil praised the calm of the abbey of Châlis and Nicholas
of Clémanges the tranquility of the priory of Fontaine-au-Bois.
They found St Bernard's "inner man" there – but along with
Cicero and Horace. "Fleeing the pomp of courts and the tumult
of cities, you will live in the country, you will love solitude," said
Jean de Montreuil.

And here is the beginning of *The Godly Feast* by Erasmus:

EUSEBIUS:	Now that the whole countryside is fresh and smiling, I marvel at people who take pleasure in smoky cities.
TIMOTHY:	Some people don't enjoy the sight of flowers or verdant meadows or fountains or streams; or if they do, something else pleases them more. Thus pleasure succeeds pleasure, as nail drives out nail.
EUSEBIUS:	Maybe you're referring to moneylenders, or greedy merchants, who are just like them.
TIMOTHY:	Those, yes, but not those alone, my good friend. No, countless others besides them, including the very priests and monks themselves, who for the sake of gain usually prefer to live in cities – the most populous cities. They follow not Pythagorean or Platonic doctrine, but that of a certain blind beggar who rejoiced in the jostling of a crowd, because (he said) where there were people, there was his profit.
EUSEBIUS:	Away with the blind and their profit! We are philosophers.
TIMOTHY:	Also the philosopher Socrates preferred cities to fields, because he was eager to learn, and cities afforded him means of learning. In the fields, to be sure, were trees and gardens, fountains and streams, that pleased the eye; but they had nothing to say, and therefore taught nothing.
EUSEBIUS:	Socrates wasn't altogether wrong, if you mean roaming in the field by yourself. In my opinion, however, Nature is not silent but talks to us all the time, on every hand, and teaches the observant man many things if she finds

him attentive and receptive. What else does the charming countenance of blooming Nature proclaim than that God the creator's wisdom is equal to his goodness? But how many things does Socrates teach his Phaedrus in that retreat, and how many learn from him in turn!

TIMOTHY: If people of that sort were present, nothing could be more enjoyable than country life.

EUSEBIUS: Then would you care to chance this? I've a little villa outside of town, a small but well-cultivated place, to which I invite you for lunch tomorrow.

TIMOTHY: There are a good many of us. We'd eat you out of house and home.

EUSEBIUS: Oh, no, you'll have a green feast made, as Horace says, "from food not bought." The place itself supplies the wine; the very trees all but drop pumpkins, melons, figs, pears, apples, and nuts into your lap, as happens (if we believe Lucian) in the Fortunate Isles. Perhaps we can have a hen from the coop.

TIMOTHY: Well, we don't decline.[10]

THE BREAK BETWEEN KNOWLEDGE AND TEACHING

Thus the humanists abandoned one of the primary tasks of the intellectual, which was to have contact with the masses, to connect their knowledge with teaching. Undoubtedly the Renaissance ultimately brought to humanity the harvest of an arrogant and solitary work. Its knowledge, its ideas, and its masterpieces ultimately fed human progress. But it was first of all a withdrawal, a recoiling. The printing press perhaps first favored – before spreading written culture everywhere – a shrinking of the diffusion of thought. Those who knew how to read were a small favored elite, and were happy that way. Others were no longer fed on crumbs from the scholasticism which had been provided them by the preachers and "artists" of the Middle Ages, all of whom were trained by the universities. It was

[10] *Ten Colloquies of Erasmus*, translated with an introduction and notes by Craig R. Thompson (New York: The Liberal Arts Press, 1957), pp. 130–2. – TRANS.

perhaps necessary to await the Counter-Reformation for an art to appear which – in a perhaps questionable form, but one full of didactic intentions and an enthusiasm for propagating new ideas – would seek to have the people participate in cultural affairs.

There is nothing more striking than the contrast between images which show the intellectual in the Middle Ages and the humanist at work. The former is a professor, caught up in his teaching, surrounded by students, besieged by benches, where his audience is pressing in. The other is a solitary scholar, in his calm chamber, at ease in the midst of the private, luxurious room where his thoughts can move freely about. The former shows the tumult of schools, the dust of classrooms, the collective worker's indifference to beauty,

> The latter shows all is order and beauty,
> Luxury, calm and pleasure.

PLATE 45　*St Jerome, by Carpaccio (Courtesy Giraudon)*

BIBLIOGRAPHY AND FURTHER READING

Compiled by David Van Meter and Richard Landes

I THE INTELLECTUAL AND CULTURAL CLIMATE OF THE MIDDLE AGES

Amos, T., ed. *De Ore Domini: Preaching and Word in the Middle Ages.* Studies on Medieval Culture 27. Kalamazoo, 1989.

Auerbach, Erich, *European Literature and the Latin Middle Ages,* tr. Willard Trask. Princeton, 1973.

Baldwin, J. W. *The Scholastic Culture of the Middle Ages. 1000–1300.* Lexington, Mass., 1971.

Beer, J. M. A. *Narrative Conventions of Truth in the Middle Ages.* Geneva, 1981.

Berman, H. J. *Law and Revolution: The Formation of the Western Legal Tradition.* Cambridge, MA, 1983.

Berschin, Walter, *Greek letters and the Latin Middle Ages: from Jerome to Nicholas of Cusa.* Tr. Jerold C. Frakes. Washington, D.C., 1988.

Bischoff, Bernhard. *Latin Paleography*: Antiquity and the Middle Ages. Tr. D. O'Croinin and David Ganz. New York, 1991.

Bloch, R. H. *Etymologies and Genealogies: A Literary Anthropology of the French Middle Ages.* Chicago, 1983.

Blumenberg. H. *The Genesis of the Copernican World.* Cambridge, MA, 1987.

Bolgar, R. B. *The Classical Heritage and its Beneficiaries.* New York, 1954, 1964.

Boswell, John, *Christianity, social tolerance, and homosexuality: Gay People in Western Europe from the beginning of the Christian era to the Fourteenth Century.* Chicago, 1980.

Burrow, J. *the Ages of Man: A Study in Medieval Writing and Thought.* Oxford, 1986.

Burns, J. H., ed. *The Cambridge History of Medieval Political Thought.* Cambridge, 1987.

Bynum, Caroline Walker, *Jesus as Mother: studies in the spirituality of the High Middle Ages*. Berkeley, 1982.

Campbell, M. B. *The Witness and the Other World: Exotic European Travel Writing, 400–1600*. Ithaca and London, 1988.

Clanchy, M. T. *From Memory to Written Record: England, 1066–1307*. London, 1979. 2 edn: Cambridge, MA and Oxford, 1992.

Copleston, F. C. *Medieval Philosophy*. London, 1952.

Curtius, E. R. *European Literature and the Latin Middle Ages*. Tr. W. R. Trask. London, 1953.

Dronke, P. *Woman Writers of the Middle Ages: A Critical Study of Texts from Perpetua to Marquerite Porete*. Cambridge, 1984.

Dronke, P. *Poetic Individuality in the Middle Ages: New Departures in Poetry, 1000–1150*. Oxford, 1970.

Duhem, P. *Medieval Cosmology: Theories of Infinity, Place, Void, and the Plurality of Worlds*. Ed. and tr. R. Ariew. Chicago, 1985.

Eco, U. *Art and Beauty in the Middle Ages*. Translated by H. Bredin. New Haven, 1986.

Gilson, E. *History of Christian Philosophy in the Middle Ages*, New York, 1955.

Grundmann, "Litteratus-illiteratus der Wandlung einer Bildungsnorm von Altertum zum Mittelalter," *Archiv für Kulturges-chichte* 40 (1958), 1–65.

Gurevich, A. *Categories of Medieval Culture*. Tr. G. L. Campbell. London, 1985.

Gurevich, A. *Medieval Popular Culture: Problems of Belief and Perception*. Tr. J. Bak and P. Hollingsworth. New York, 1990.

Hardison, O. B., Jr., ed. *Medieval Literary Criticism: Translations and Interpretations*. New York, 1974.

Head, Thomas. *Haqiography and Cult of the Saints in the Diocese of Orleans, 800–1200. Cambridge Studies in Medieval Life and Thought* fourth series, vol. 11. Cambridge, 1990.

Herren, M. *The Sacred Nectar of the Greeks: the Study of Greek in the West in the Early Middle Ages*. Kings College Medieval Studies, 2. London, 1988.

Hughes, A. *Medieval Music: The Sixth Liberal Art*. Toronto, 1974.

Huot, S. *From Song to Book: The Poetics of Writing in Old French Lyric and Lyrical Narrative Poetry*. Ithaca, 1987.

Jaeger, Stephen C. *The Origins of Courtliness: Civilizing Trends and the Formation of Courtly Ideals, 939–1210*. Philadelphia, 1985.

Knowles, D. *The Evolution of Medieval Thought*. Baltimore, 1962.

Kuttner, S. *Harmony from Dissonance: An Interpretation of Medieval Canon Law*. Latrobe, 1960.

Ladner, Gerhart Burian, *The idea of reform; its impact on Christian thought and action in the age of the Fathers.* Cambridge, MA, 1959.

Laistner, M. L. W. *Thought and Letters in Western Europe, A.D. 500–900.* London, 1957.

Lapidge, M. and H. Gneuss, eds. *Learning and Literature in Anglo-Saxon England: Studies Presented to Peter Clemoes on the Occasion of his Sixty-Fifth Birthday.* Cambridge, 1985.

Leclerq, J. *The Love of Learning and the Desire for God: A Study of Monastic Culture.* Tr. C. Marsh. New York, 1961.

Leff, G. *Medieval Thought.* Harmondsworth, 1950.

Le Goff, J. *Time, Work and Culture in the Middle Ages.* Tr. Arthur Goldhammer. Chicago, 1980.

Le Goff, J. *The Medieval Imagination.* Tr. Arthur Goldhammer. Chicago, 1988.

Le Goff, J. *Medieval Civilization.* Tr. Julia Barrow. Oxford and Cambridge MA, 1988.

Leyser, Henrietta, *Hermits and the New Monasticism: A Study of Religious Communities in Western Europe, 1000–1150.* London 1984.

Little, L. K. *Religious Poverty and the Profit Economy in Medieval Europe.* London, 1978.

Makdisi, G. "The Scholastic Method in Medieval Education: An Inquiry into its Origins in Law and Theology." *Speculum* 4 (1974): 640–661.

McGinn, Bernard. *Visions of the End: Apocalyptic Traditions in the Middle Ages.* New York, 1979.

McKitterick, R., ed. *The Uses of Literacy in Early Medieval Europe.* Cambridge, 1990.

McKitterick, R. *The Carolingians and the Written Word.* Cambridge, 1989.

Meyvaert, Paul, *Benedict, Gregory, Bede and Others.* London, reissued 1977.

Morrall, J. B. *Political Thought in Medieval Times.* London, 1960.

Colin Morris. *The Papal Monarchy: The Western Church from 1050 to 1250.* Oxford, 1989.

Morrison, Karl Frederick, *The Mimetic Tradition of Reform in the West.* Princeton, 1982.

Morrison, Karl Frederick, *I Am You: The Hermeneutics of Empathy in Western Literature, Theology, and Art.* Princeton, 1988.

Muir, L. R. *Literature and Society in Medieval France: The Mirror and the Image, 1100–1500.* New York, 1985.

Murray, A. *Reason and Society in the Middle Ages.* Oxford, 1978.

Murdoch, J. E., and E. D. Sylla, eds. *The Cultural Context of Medieval Learning: Proceedings of the First International Colloquium on Philosophy, Science and Technology in the Middle Ages. Boston Studies in the Philosophy of Science* 26. Dordrecht-Boston, 1975.

Murphy, J. J. *Rhetoric in the Middle Ages: A History of Rhetorical Theory from Augustine to the Renaissance.* Berkeley, 1974.

Panofsky, E. *Gothic Architecture and Scholasticism.* Latrobe, 1951.

Partner, N. *Serious Entertainments: The Writing of History in Twelfth Century England.* Chicago, 1977.

Paxton, Frederick S. *Christianizing Death : The Creation of a Ritual Process in Early Medieval Europe.* Ithaca, 1990.

Radding, C. *A World Made by Men: Cognition and Society, 400–1200.* Chapel Hill, 1985.

Reese, G. *Music in the Middle Ages.* New York, 1940.

Reynolds, L. D. and N. G. Wilson. *Scribes and Scholars: A Guide to the Transmission of Greek and Latin Literature.* Oxford, 1968.

Riché, Pierre. *Education and Culture in the Barbarian West, Sixth through Eighth Centuries.* Tr. John J. Contreni. columbia, 1976.

Saenger, P. "Silent Reading: Its Impact on Late Medieval Script and Society." *Viator* 1982: 367–414.

Sears, E. *The Ages of Man: Medieval Interpretations of the Life Cycle.* Princeton, 1986.

Smalley, B. *The Becket Controversy and the Schools: A Study of Intellectuals in Politics.* London, 1973.

Smalley, B. *Historians in the Middle Ages.* London, 1974.

Smalley, B. *The Study of the Bible in the Middle Ages.* Oxford, 1952.

Stock, B. *The Implications of Literacy: Written Language and Models of Interpretation in the Eleventh and Twelfth Centuries.* Princeton, 1983.

Straw, Carole Ellen, *Gregory the Great: Perfection in Imperction.* Berkeley, 1988.

Thorndike, L. "Elementary and Secondary Education in the Middle Ages." *Speculum* 15 (1940): 400–408.

Ullman, W. *A History of Political Thought: The Middle Ages.* Baltimore, 1965.

Verbeke, W., D. Verhelst, and A Welkenhuysen, eds. *The Use and Abuse of Eschatology in the Middle Ages.* Leuven, 1988.

Vance, E. *Mervelous Signals: Poetics and Sign Theory in the Middle Ages.* Lincoln, NE, 1986.

Vitz, Evelyn Birge, *Medieval Narrative and Modern Narratology: Subjects and Objects of Desire* New York, 1989.

Waddell, H. *The Wandering Scholars.* 7th edition, London, 1934.

Ward, Benedicta. *Miracles and the Medieval Mind: Theory, Record and Event, 1000–1215.* Philadelphia, 1982.

Weisheipl, J. A. "Classification of the Sciences in Medieval Thought." *Medieval Studies* 1965: 27.

White, L. *Medieval Religion and Technology: Collected Essays. Center for Medieval and Renaissance Studies* 13. Berkeley, 1978.

Williams, John, and Alison Stones, eds. *The Codex Calixtinus and the Shrine of St. James.* Tübingen, 1992.

II INTELLECTUAL EFFORTS PRIOR
TO THE UNIVERSITIES

Allott, S. *Alcuin of York.* York, 1974.

Babcock, R. G., *Heriger of Lobbes and the Freising Florileqium: A Study of the Influence of Classical Latin Poetry in the Middle Ages. Lateinische Sprache und Literatur des Mittelalters* 18. Frankfurt and New York, 1984.

Baldwin, J. W. *Masters, Princes and Merchants: The Social Views of Peter the Chanter and his Circle.* Princeton, 1970, 2 vols.

Barker, L. K. "Ivo of Chartres and the Anglo-Norman Cultural Tradition." *Anglo-Norman Studies* 13 (1990): 15–33.

Barrow, J. S., C. S. F. Burnett and D. E. Luscombe, eds. "A Check-list of the Manuscripts Containing Writings of Peter Abelard and Heloise and of Other Works Closely Associated With Abelard and his School." *Revue d'histoire des textes* 14–15 (1984–85): 183–302.

Benson, R. L. and G. Constable, eds. *Renaissance and Renewal in the XIIth Century.* Cambridge, MA. 1982.

Benton, J. F., ed. *Self and Society in Medieval France: The Memoirs of Abbot Guibert of Nogent.* Tr. by C. C. Swinton. Toronto, 1984.

Bischoff, B. "Turning Points in the History of Latin Exegesis in the Early Middle Ages." *Biblical Studies: The Medieval Irish Contribution.* Ed. M. McNamara. Dublin, 1976: 73–160.

Bloch, R. H. *Scandal of the Fabliaux.* Chicago, 1986.

Brownlee, M., Brownlee, K., and Nichols, S., eds. *The New Medievalism.* Baltimore and London, 1991: 226–249.

Buc, Philippe, "David's Adultery with Bathsheba and the Healing Powers of the Capetian King," *Viator* 24 (1993)

Burnett, C. S. F., ed. *Adelard of Bath: An English Scientist and Arabist of the Early Twelfth Century.* London, 1987.

Carre, H. M. *Realists and Nominalists.* Oxford, 1946.

Chenu, M.-D., *Nature, Man and Society in the Twelfth Century: Essays on the New Theological Perspectives in the Latin West.* Tr. J. Taylor and L. K. Little. Chicago, 1968.

Chodorow, S. *Christian Political Theory and Church Politics in the Mid-Twelfth Century.* Berkeley, 1972.

Clagett, M. et al., eds. *Twelfth-Century Europe and the Foundations of Modern Society.* Madison, 1961.

Edyvean, W. *Anselm of Havelberg and the Theology of History.* Rome, 1972.

Evans, G. R. *The Language and Logic of the Bible: The Earlier Middle Ages.* Cambridge, 1984.

Evans, G. R. "The Development of Some Textbooks on the Useful Arts, ca. 1000–1250." *History of Education* 7 (1978): 85–94.

Flint, V. I. J. "The School of Laon: A Reconsideration." *Recherces de Theologie ancienne et medievale* 43 (1976): 89–110.

Flint, V. I. J. *The rise of magic in early medieval Europe.* Princeton, 1991.

Gibson, M. *Lanfranc of Bec.* Oxford, 1978.

Gilson, E. *The Mystical Theology of Saint Bernard.* London, 1950.

Häring, N. M. "Chartres and Paris Revisited." *Essays in Honour of Auton Charles Pegis.* Toronto, 1974.

Kristeller, P.O. "The School of Salerno: Its Development and its Contribution to the History of Learning." *Bull. Hist. Medicine* 17 (1945).

Kuttner, Stephan. *The History of Ideas and Doctrines of Canon Law in the Middle Ages.* London, 1980.

MacKinney, H. C. *Bishop Fulbert and Education at the School of Chartres.* University of Notre Dame, 1957.

Marrenbon, J. *From the Circle of Alcuin to the School of Auxerre: Logic, Theology and Philosophy in the Early Middle Ages.* Cambridge, 1981.

Marrenbon, J. *Early Medieval Philosophy (480–1150): An Introduction,* 2nd edn. New York, 1988.

McGarry, D. *The Metalogicon of John of Salisbury.* Gloucester, Mass., 1971.

Moore, R. I. *The Formation of a Persecuting Society: Power and Deviance in Western Europe, 950–1250.* Oxford and Cambridge MA, 1987.

Morris, C. *The Discovery of the Individual, 1050–1200.* London, 1972.

Morrison, K. F. *Tradition and Authority in the Western Church, 300–1140.* Princeton, 1969.

Mostert, M. *The Political Theology of Abbo of Fleury: A Study of the Ideas about Society and the Law of the Tenth-century Monastic Reform Movement.* Middeleeuwse Studies en Bronnen 2. Hilversum, 1987.

Nichols, Stephen G. Jr., *Romanesque Signs, Early Medieval Narrative and Iconography,* New Haven, 1983.

Post, G. "Alexander III, The 'Licentia Docendi' and the Rise of Universities." *Anniversary Essays in Medieval History by the Students of C. H. Haskins.* Boston and New York, 1929: 255–277.

Reinsma, L. M. "Rhetoric, Grammar, and Literature in England and Ireland Before the Norman Conquest: a Select Bibliography." *Rhetoric Society Quarterly* 8.1 (1978): 29–48.

Reynolds, R. E. "Liturgical Scholarship at the Time of the Investiture Controversy: Past Research and Future Opportunities." *Harvard Theological Review* 70 (1978): 109–124.

Riché, Pierre. *Education and Culture in the Barbarian West, Sixth through Eighth Centuries.* Tr. John J. contreni. columbia, 1976.

Robinson, I. S. *Authority and Resistance in the Investiture Contest: The Polemical Literature of the Late Eleventh Century.* Manchester, 1978.

Schmid, Karl. *Education and Culture in the Barbarian West.* Columbia, S. C., 1976.

Schriber, C. P. *The Dilemma of Arnulf of Lisieux: New Ideas versus Old Ideals.* Bloomington, 1990.

Southern, R. W. *Medieval Humanism and Other Essays.* Oxford, 1970.

Southern, R. W. *Platonism, Scholastic Method and the School of Chartres.* Stenton Lecture, University of Reading, 1979.

Southern, R. W. *St. Anselm and his Biographer.* Cambridge, 1963.

Vance, E. *From Topos to Tale: Logic and Narrativity in the Middle Ages.* Minneapolis, 1987.

van Engen, J. *Rupert of Deutz.* Berkeley, 1983.

Vicaire, M. -H. *Saint Dominic and his Times.* London, 1964.

Wilks, M., ed. *The World of John of Salisbury. Studies in Church History,* Subsidia III, Oxford and Cambridge, MA, 1984.

Williams, J. R. "The Cathedral School of Reims in the Time of Master Alberic, 1118–1136." *Traditio* 20 (1964): 93–114.

Wolff, P. *The Awakening of Europe.* Tr. Anne Carter. New York, 1968.

Zinn, G. A. "Hugh of St. Victor and the Art of Memory." *Viator* 5 (1974).

Ziolkowski, J. *Alan of Lille's Grammar of Sex: The Meaning of Grammar to a Twelfth Century Intellectual.* Cambridge, MA, 1985.

III GENERAL STUDIES OF MEDIEVAL UNIVERSITIES

1 Bibliographies

Bibliographie internationale de l'histoire des Université; I. Espagne, Louvain-Copenhague-Prague. Études et documents publiés par la section d'histoire de la faculté des lettres de l'Université de Genève, 9. Geneva, 1973.

Gabriel, A. L. *Summary Bibliography of the History of the Universities of Great Britain and Ireland up to 1800.* University of Notre Dame, 1974.

Guenée, S. *Bibliographie d'histoire des Universités françaises des origines à la Revolution.* Vol. I: *Generalités et Univeristé de Paris.* Paris, 1981. Vol. II: *D'Aix-en-Provence à Valence et Académies protestantes.* Paris, 1988.

Stelling-Michaud, S. "L'histoire des Universités au Moyen Age et à la Renaissance au cours des vingt-cinq dernière années." *Rapports du XIe Congrès international des sciences historiques.* Stockholm, I, 1960.

2   General Works on the Medieval Universities

Cobban, A. B. *The Medieval Universities: Their Development and Organization.* London, 1975.

d'Irsay, S. *Histoire des universités françaises et étrangères des origines à nos jours,* vol. 1: *Le Moyen Age et la Renaissance.* Paris, 1933.

Matthew, A. *Schools and Universities on the Continent.* London, 1868.

Orme, N. *Education in the West of England, 1066–1548.* Exeter, 1976.

Orme, N. *English Schools in the Middle Ages.* London, 1973.

Rashdall, H. *The Universities of Europe in the Middle Ages.* 3 vols, Oxford, 1936.

Wieruszowski, H. *The Medieval University.* New York, 1966.

3   The Origins of the Medieval University

Ferruolo, Stephen C., *The Origins of the University: The Schools of Paris and their Critics, 1100–1215* Stanford 1985.

Grundmann, H. *Vom Ursprung der Universität im Mittelalter.* Berlin, 1957.

Haskins, C. H. *The Rise of Universities.* Ithaca, 1923, 1962.

Post, G. "Alexander III, the 'Licentia docendi', and the Rise of Universities." In *Anniversary Essays in Medieval History by Students of Charles Homer Haskins.* Boston, 1929: 255–277.

Radding, Charles. *The Origins of Medieval Jurisprudence: Pavia and Bologna, 850–1150.* New Haven, 1988.

4   Documentation and General Aspects

Gabriel, A. L. *Garlandia: Studies in the History of the Medieval University.* Frankfurt, 1969.

Gabriel, A. L. "The Ideal Master of the Medieval University." *The Catholic Historical Review* 60 (1974).

Leach, A. F. *Educational Charters and Documents.* Cambridge, 1911.

Michaud-Quantin, P. *Universitas. Expressions du mouvement communautaire dans le Moyen Age Latin.* Paris, 1970.

Post, G., K. Giocarinis and R. Kay. "The Medieval Heritage of a Humanistic Ideal: 'Scientia donum dei est, unde vendi non potest'." *Traditio* 11 (1955).

5 Comparative Studies

Agus, Jacob B. *The Evolution of Jewish Thought from Biblical Times to the Opening of the Modern Era.* New York, 1959.

Baron, Salo, *The Jewish Community.* 3 vols, New York, 1948.

Makdisi, G. "Madrasa and University in the Middle Ages." *Studia Islamica* (1970): 255–264.

Needham, J. *Clerks and Craftsmen in China and the West.* Cambridge, 1970.

Sherrard, Ph. *The Greek East and the Latin West: A Study in the Christian Tradition.* London, 1959.

South, M. T. *Li Ho: A Scholar-Official of the Yuan-ho Period (860–821).* Leyde, 1959.

IV UNIVERSITIES AND SCHOLARS, PARTICULARLY OF THE THIRTEENTH CENTURY

Aston, T. H. "The Medieval Alumni of the University of Cambridge." *Past and Present* 86 (1980): 9–86.

Aston, T. H. "Oxford's Medieval Alumni." *Past and Present* 74 (1977).

Baldwin, J. W. "Masters at Paris from 1179 to 1215: A Social Perspective." *Renaissance and Renewal in the XIIth Century.* Cambridge, MA, 1982.

Baldwin, J. H. "'Studium et Regnum': The Penetration of University Personnel into French and English Administration at the Turn of the Twelfth and Thirteenth Centuries." *Revue des Etudes Islamiques* 44: *l'Enseignement en Islam et en Occident au Moyen Age* (1976).

Beaujouan, G. "Motives and Opportunities for Science in the Medieval Universities." In *Scientific Change* ed. A. C. Combie. London, 1963.

Bernstein, A. E. "Magisterium and license: Corporative Autonomy against Papal Authority in the Medieval University of Paris." *Viator* 9 (1978): 291–307.

Bloch, H. "Monte Cassino's Teachers and Library in the High Middle Ages." In *La scuola nell'Occidente latino dell'alto medioevo*, II. Spoleto, 1972: 563–605.

Bloch, H. *Monte Cassino in the Middle Ages.* 3 vols, Cambridge, Mass., 1986.

Boyce, G. C. *The English German Nation in the University of Paris during the Middle Ages*. Bruges, 1927.

Bullough, V. L. *The Development of Medicine as a Profession*. New York, 1966.

Cobban, A. B. "The Medieval Cambridge Colleges: A Quantitative Study of Higher Degrees to circa 1500." *History of Education* 9 (1980).

Cobban, A. B. "Medieval Student Power." *Past and Present* 53 (1971): 28–66.

Cuton, J. I., ed. *The History of the University of Oxford, I. The Early Oxford Schools*. Oxford, 1983.

Dunbabin, J. "Aristotle's *Politics:* Reception and Interpretation." In *The Cambridge History of Later Medieval Philosophy*. Ed. N. Kretzmann, A. Kenny and J. Pinborg. Cambridge, 1982: 723–737.

Emden, A. B. *A Bibliographical Register of the University of Cambridge to A.D. 1500*. Cambridge, 1963.

Emden, A.B. *A Bibliographical Register of the University of Oxford to A.D. 1500*. 3 vols, Oxford, 1957.

Gabriel, A. L. "The Economic and Material Frame of the Medieval Universities." In *Texts and Studies in the History of Medieval Education* 15. University of Notre Dame, 1977.

Gabriel, A. L. "The Source of the Anecdote of the Inconstant Scholar." *Classica et Mediaevalia* 19. Copenhagen, 1958.

Haskins, C. H. "The Life of Medieval Students as Illustrated by their Letters;" "The University of Paris in the Sermons of the 13th Century;" and "Manuals for Students." In *Studies in Material Culture*. New York, 1929: 1–91.

Hays, R. W. "Welsh Students at Oxford and Cambridge Universities in the Middle Ages." *Welsh Historical Review* 4 (1968–69): 325–361.

Kantorowicz, E. "The Prologue to *Fleta* and the School of Petrus de Vinea." *Speculum* 32 (1957): 231–249.

Kibre, P. *The Nations in the Medieval Universities*. Cambridge, Mass., 1948.

Kibre, P. *Scholarly Privileges in the Middle Ages: The Rights, Privileges and Immunities of Scholars and Universities at Bologna, Padua, Paris and Oxford*. London, 1962.

Kristeller, P.O. "The School of Salerno." *Bulletin of the History of Medicine* 17 (1945): 138–194.

Lawrence, C. H. "Stephen of Lexington and Cistercian University Studies in the Thirteenth Century." *Journal of Ecclesiastical History* 11 (1960): 164–178.

Leff, G. *Paris and Oxford Universities in the Thirteenth and Fourteenth Centuries*. New York, 1968.

MacLaughlin, M. M. *Intellectual Freedom and its Limitations in the University of Paris in the XIIIth and XIVth Centuries.* New York, 1977.

Martin, C. "Some Medieval Commentaries on Aristotle's *Politics.*" *History* 36 (1951): 29–44.

Murphy, J. J. "The Earliest Teaching of Rhetoric at Oxford." *Speech Monographs* 27 (1960): 345–347.

Paetow, L. J. *The Arts Course at Medieval Universities, with Special Reference to Grammar and Rhetoric.* Champaign, 1910.

Pollard, P. "The Pecia System in the Medieval Universities." *Medieval Scribes, Manuscripts and Libraries: Essays Presented to N. R. Ker.* London, 1978: 145–161.

Post, G. "Masters' Salaries and Student Fees in the Medieval Universities." *Speculum* 7 (1932): 181–190.

Post, G. "Parisian Masters as a Corporation, 1200–1246." *Speculum* 9 (1934): 421–445.

Powicke, E. M. *Ways of Medieval Life and Thought.* London, 1950.

Rouse, R. H. "The Early Library of the Sorbonne." *Scriptorium* 21 (1967): 42–71 and 227–51.

Siraisi, N. G. *Arts and Sciences at Padua: The Studium of Padua before 1350.* Toronto, 1973.

Smith, C. E. *The University of Toulouse in the Middle Ages.* Milwaukee, 1959.

Stephany, W. "Pier Della Vigna's Self-Fulfilling Prophecies: The *Eulogy* of Frederick II and *Inferno* 13." *Traditio* 38 (1982): 193–212.

Talbot, C. H. "The English Cistercians and the Universities." *Los Monjes y los estudios.* Poblet, 1963.

Temko, A. *Notre-Dame of Paris.* New York, 1955, 1967.

Thorndike, L. *University Records and Life in the Middle Ages.* New York, 1949.

Wagner, D., ed. *The Seven Liberal Arts in the Middle Ages.* Bloomington, 1983.

Watt, D. E. R. *A Biographical Dictionary of Scottish Graduates to A.D. 1410.* Oxford and New York, 1977.

Weisheipol, J. A. "Curriculum of the Faculty of Arts at Oxford in the Early XIVth Century." *Medieval Studies* 26 (1964): 154–56 and 177–81.

Wieruszowski, H. "Arezzo as a Center of Learning and Letters in the Thirteenth Century." *Traditio* 9 (1953): 321–391.

V INTELLECTUAL PROBLEMS AND DEBATES
OF THE THIRTEENTH CENTURY

Boyle, L. E. "The Quodlibets of St. Thomas and Pastoral Care." *The Thomist* 38 (1974): 232–256.

David Burr, *Franciscan Poverty: The Origins of the Usus Pauper Controversy* (Philadelphia: University of Pennsylvania Press, c1989).

Callus, D. A. "The Introduction of Aristotelean Learning to Oxford." *Proceedings of the British Academy* 29 (1943): 229–281.

Eckenrode, T. R. "Vincent of Beauvais: A Study on the Construction of a Didactic View of History." *Historian* 46 (1984): 339–360.

Ferrante, J. *Woman as Image in Medieval Literature from the Twelfth Century to Dante*. New York, 1975.

Flemming, J. V. *From Bonaventure to Bellini: An Essay in Franciscan Exegesis*. Princeton, 1982.

Flood, D. *Peter Olivi's Rule Commentary*. Wiesbaden, 1972.

Fowler, G. B. *Intellectual Interests of Engelbert of Admont*. New York, 1947.

Funkenstein, Amos, *Theology and the scientific imagination from the Middle Ages to the seventeenth century*. Princeton 1986.

Gabriel, A. L. *The Educational Ideas of Vincent of Beauvais. Texts and Studies in the History of Medieval Education* 4. Notre Dame, 1956.

Gilson, E. *Reason And Revelation in the Middle Ages*. New York 1938.

Goetz, M. P. *The Concept of Nobility in German Didactic Literature of the Thirteenth Century. Catholic University of America: Studies in German* 5. Washington, D.C., 1935.

Goodich, M. *Vita Perfecta: The Ideal of Sainthood in the Thirteenth Century*. Stuttgart, 1982.

Griffiths, Q. "New Men Among the Lay Counselors of Saint Louis' Parlement." *Mediaeval Studies* 32 (1970): 234–272.

Lee, Harold, Marjorie Reeves, Giulio Silano, *Western Mediterranean Prophecy: The School of Joachim of Fiore and the Fourteenth-century Breviloquium*. Toronto 1989.

Leff, G. *The Dissolution of the Medieval Outlook: An Essay on Intellectual and Spiritual Change in the Fourteenth Century*. New York 1976.

Lerner, R. E. *The Heresy of the Free Spirit in the Later Middle Ages*. Berkeley, 1972.

Maier, Anneliese, *On the Threshold of Exact Science: Selected Writings of Anneliese Maier on Late Medieval Natural Philosophy*. Ed. and tr. Steven D. Sargent. Philadelphia, 1982.

Marrenbon, J. *Later Medieval Philosophy (1150–1350): An Introduction*. London and New York, 1987.

Marone, S. P. *William of Auvergne and Robert Grosseteste: New Ideals of Truth in the Early XIIIth Century*. Princeton, 1983.

McCarthy, J. M. *Humanistic Emphases in the Educational Thought of Vincent of Beauvais. Studien und Texte zur Geistesgeschichte des Mittelalters* 10. Leiden, 1976.

Moorman, J. R. H. *A History of the Franciscan Order.* Oxford, 1968.

Murray, A. "Piety and Impiety in Thirteenth Century Italy." In *Popular Belief and Practice.* Ed. J. Cuming and D. Baker. Cambridge, 1972.

Neel, C. "Man's Restoration: Robert of Auxerre and the Writing of History in the Early Thirteenth Century." *Traditio* 44 (1988): 253–274.

Noonan, J. T. *The Scholastic Analysis of Usury.* Cambridge, MA 1957.

Peters, F. E. *Aristotle and the Arabs.* New York, 1968.

Post, G., K. Giocarnis, and R. Kay. "The Medieval Heritage of a Humanistic Ideal: 'Scientia donum dei est, unde vendi non potest.'" *Traditio* 11 (1955): 209–10.

Purcell, M. "Changing Views of the Crusade in the Thirteenth Century." *Journal of Religious History* 2 (1972): 3–20.

Reeves, M. *Joachim of Fiore and the Prophetic Future.* London, 1976.

Riley-Smith, J. S. C. "An Approach to Crusading Ethics." *Reading Medieval Studies* 6 (1980): 3–20.

Roensch, F. J. *The Early Thomistic School.* Dubuque, 1964.

Russell, F. H. *The Just War in the Middle Ages.* Cambridge, 1975.

Sharp, D. E. *Franciscan Philosophy at Oxford.* Oxford, 1930.

Siberry, E. *Criticisms of Crusading, 1095–1274.* Oxford, 1985.

Slattery, M. *Myth, Man and Sovereign Saint: King Louis IX in Joinville's Source.* New York, 1985.

Tuilier, A. "La renaissance de l'aristotelisme universitaire a Paris au XIIIe siecle." *The Cambridge History of Later Medieval Philosophy: from Rediscovery of Aristotle to the Disintegration of Scholasticism, 1100–1600.* Cambridge, 1982: 7–21.

Van Steenberghen, F. *Aristotle in the West: The Origins of Latin Aristotelianism.* Louvain, 1955.

Wei, I. P. "Guy de l'Aumone's 'Summa de Diversis Questionibus Theologie'." *Traditio* 44 (1988): 275–323.

Weisheipl, J. *The Development of Physical Theory in the Middle Ages.* London, 1959.

Weisheipl, J. "The Principle 'Omne quod movetur ab alio movetur' in Medieval Physics." *Isis* 56 (1965): 26–45.

West, D. E. "The Education of Fra Salimbene of Parma: The Joachite Influence." In *Prophecy and Millenarianism: Essays in Honour of M. Reeves* ed. A. Williams. London, 1980.

Wippel, J. F. "Quodlibetal Questions, chiefly in Theological Facilities." In *Les Questiones disputées et les questiones quod libetiques dans les facultes de theologie, de droit et de medecin.* Turnhout, 1985.

Wippel, J. F. "The Quodlibetal Question as a Distinctive Literary Genre." In *Les Genres littéraires dans les sources théologiques et philosophiques médiévales:*

definition, critique et exposition. Actes du Colloque Internationale de Louvain-la-Neuve 25–27 mai 1981. Louvain-la-Neuve, 1982: 67–84.

VI UNIVERSITIES AND SCHOLARS OF THE FOURTEENTH AND FIFTEENTH CENTURIES: MEDIEVAL INTELLECTUALS AND HUMANISTS

Baldwin, J. W. and R. A. Goldthwaite, eds. *Universities in Politics: Case Studies from the Later Middle Ages and Early Modern Period.* Baltimore and London, 1972.

Bell, S. "Christine de Pizan [1364–1430]: Humanism and the Problem of a Studious Woman." *Feminist Studies* 3 (1976).

Bernstein, A. E. "Esoteric Theology: William of Auvergne on the Fires of Hell and Purgatory." *Speculum* 57 (1982): 509–531.

Bernstein, A. E. *Pierre d'Ailly and the Blanchard Affair: University and Chancellor of Paris at the Beginning of the Great Schism.* Leyde, 1978.

Blumenberg, H. "Aspects of the Epochal Threshold: The Cusan and the Nolan." In *The Legitimacy of the Modern Age.* Tr. R. M. Wallace. Cambridge, MA, 1983.

Bouwsma, W. J. *The Interpretation of Renaissance Humanism.* Washington, D.C., 1959.

Buhler, C. F. *The University and the Press in XVth Century Bologna.* Indiana University Press, 1958.

Butler, P. *The Origins of Printing in Europe.* Chicago, 1940.

Cam, H. *Law-finders and Law-makers in Medieval England.* New York, 1963.

Campbell, A. M. *The Black Death and Men of Learning.* New York, 1931.

Chaney, E. F. *Francois Villon in His Environment.* Oxford, 1946.

Clarke, M. L. *Classical Education in Britain, 1500–1900.* Cambridge, 1959.

Coogan, R., tr. and ed. *Babylon on the Thone: A Translation of Letters by Dante, Petrarch, and Catherine of Sienna on the Avignon Papacy.* Madrid, 1983.

Courtenay, W. J. *Adam Wodeham.* Leiden, 1978.

Courtenay, W. J. "The Effect of the Black Death on English Higher Education." *Speculum* 55 (1980): 696–714.

Davis, C. T. *Dante and the Idea of Rome.* Oxford, 1957.

Dunbabin, J. "Guido Vernani of Rimini's Commentary on Aristotle's *Politics.*" *Traditio* 44 (1988): 373–388.

Ermatinger, Ch. J. "Averroism in Early Fourteenth Century Bologna." *Medieval Studies* 16 (1954).

Gabriel, A. L. "The College System in the XIVth Century Universities." In *The Forward Movement of the XIVth Century* ed. F. L. Utley. Columbus, 1961: 79–124.

Gabriel, A. L. *Petrus Cesaris Wagner and Johannes Stoll: XIVth Century Printers at the University of Paris.* University of Notre Dame, 1978.

Gabriel, A. L. "Student Life in Ave Maria College, Medieval Paris." In *History and Chartulary of the College.* University of Notre Dame, 1955.

Gewirth, A. "John of Jandun and the *Defensor Pacis.*" *Speculum* 23 (1948): 267–272.

Gewirth, A. *Marsilius of Padua.* 2 vols, New York, 1951–56.

Greene, T. M. *The Light in Troy: Imitation and Discovery in Renaissance Poetry.* New Haven, 1982.

Hargreaves, H. "Popularising Biblical Scholarship: the Role of the Wycliffite *Glossed Gospels.*" In *The Bible and Medieval Culture* ed. W. Lourdaux and D. Verhelst. Louvain, 1979.

Hay, D. *The Italian Renaissance in its Historical Background.* Cambridge, 1961.

Hudson, A. Hudson. *The Premature Reformation: Wycliffite Texts and Lollard History.* Oxford, 1988.

Hutton, E. *Giovanni Boccacio: A Biographical Study.* London, 1910.

Hyde, J. K. *Padua in the Age of Dante.* Manchester, 1966.

Hyma, A. *The Bretheren of the Common Life.* Grand Rapids, 1950.

Jacob, E. F. "On the Promotion of English University Clerks during the Later Middle Ages." *Journal of Ecclesiastical History* 1 (1950).

Jarret, B. *Social Theories of the Middle Ages, 1200–1500.* London, 1926.

Kennedy, A. J. *Christine de Pizan: A Bibliographical Guide.* London, 1984.

Kirshner, J. "*Ars imitatur naturam*: A Consilium of Baldus on Naturalization in Florence." *Viator* 5 (1974): 289–331.

Kristeller, P.O. "Humanism and Scholasticism in the Italian Renaissance." *Studies in Renaissance Thought and Letters.* Rome, 1956.

Kristeller, P.O. "The University of Bologna and the Renaissance." *Studi e Memorie per la storia dell'Universita di Bologna,* n.s. 1 (1956).

Leach, A. F. *Schools of Medieval England.* Cambridge, 1915.

Leff, G. *The Dissolution of the Medieval Outlook: An Essay on Intellectual and Spiritual Change in the XIVth Century.* New York, 1976.

Lytle, G. "Patronage Patterns and Oxford Colleges, c. 1300–1530." In *The University in Society* ed. Lawrence Stone. Princeton, 1974.

Lytle, G. *Oxford Students and English Society, c. 1300–1510.* Princeton Ph.D. Dissertation, 1975.

Marti, B. M. *The Spanish College at Bologna in the Fourteenth Century: Edition and Translation of its Statutes with Introduction and Notes.* Philadelphia, 1966.

Mazzotta, G. *The World at Play in Boccacio's 'Decameron'.* Princeton, 1986.

Mommsen, T. E. "Petrarch's Conception of the Dark Ages." *Speculum* 17 (1942): 226–242.

Moody, A. Ockham, Buridan and Nicholas of Autrecourt: The Parisian Statutes of 1339 and 1340." *Franciscan Studies* 7 (1947): 113–146.

Murphy, J. J. "A New Look at Chaucer and the Rhetoricians." *Review of English Studies* n.s. 15 (1964): 1–20.

Murphy, J. J. "Rhetoric in Fourteenth Century Oxford." *Medium Aevum* 34 (1965): 1–20.

Nelson, W., ed. *A Fifteenth Century School Book*. Oxford, 1956.

Orme, N. "An Early-Tudor Oxford Schoolbook." *Renaissance Quarterly* 34 (1981).

Orme, N. "Schoolmasters, 1307–1509." In *Profession, Vocation and Culture in Medieval England* ed. C. H. Clough. Liverpool, 1982.

Parkes, M. "The Influence of the Concepts of *Ordinatio* and *Compilatio* on the Development of the Book." In *Medieval Learning and Literature: Essays Presented to William Hunt* ed. J. J. G. Alexander and M. T. Gibson. Oxford, 1976.

Pegues, F. *The Lawyers of the Last Capetians*. Princeton, 1962.

Reeves, M. *The Influence of Prophecy in the Later Middle Ages: A Study of Joachimism*. Oxford, 1969.

Robbins, R. H. "Medical Manuscripts in Middle English." *Speculum* 45 (1970): 393–415.

Salter, E. F. *Piers Plowman: An Introduction*. Oxford, 1969.

Siberry, E. "Criticism of Crusading in Fourteenth Century England." In *Crusade and Settlement* ed. P. W. Edbury. Cardiff, 1985.

Spinka, M. *John Huss: A Biography*. Princeton, 1968.

Stone, L., ed. *The University in Society, I. Oxford and Cambridge from the XIVth to the early XIXth Century*. Princeton, 1974.

Swanson, R. N. "Universities, Acadamies and the Great Schism." *Cambridge Studies in Medieval Life and Thought*. Cambridge, 1979, series 3, vol. 2.

Thorndike, L. "Renaissance or Prenaissance." *Journal of the History of Ideas* 4 (1943): 65–74.

Tierney, B. *The Origins of Papal Infallibility*. Leiden, 1972.

Tierney, B. *Foundations of the Conciliar Theory: The Contribution of the Medieval Canonists from Gratian to the Great Schism*. London, 1968.

Uitti, K. "From 'Clerc' to 'Poete': The Relevance of the *Romance of the Rose* to Machaut's World." In *Machaut's World: Science and Art in the Fourteenth Century. Annals of the New York Academy of Sciences* 314 (1978): 212–15.

van Zijl, T. *Gerard Groote: Ascetic and Reformer*. Washington, D.C., 1963.

Willard, C.C. *Christine de Pizan: Her Life and Works*. New York, 1984.

Williams, E. H. *Studies in the Life and Works of Petrarch*. Cambridge, MA, 1955.

Wilson, J. L. *A Medieval Mirror: 'Speculum humanae salvationis, 1324–1500'*. Berkeley, 1984.

Winship, G. P. *Printing in the Fifteenth Century*. Philadelphia, 1940.

Wood, R. "Adam of Wodeham on Sensory Illusions with an Edition of *Lectura Secunda*, Prologus, Quaestio 3." *Traditio* 38 (1982): 213–252.

VII SELECTED STUDIES OF EIGHTEEN OF THE GREAT INTELLECTUALS OF THE MIDDLE AGES

1 Peter Abelard (1079–1142)

Dronke, P. *Abelard and Heloise in Medieval Testimonies*. Glasgow, 1976.

Gilson, E. *Heloise and Abelard*. Chicago, 1951.

Grane, L. *Peter Abelard*. New York, 1970.

Luscombe, D. E. *Peter Abelard's Ethics*. Oxford, 1971.

Luscombe, D. E. *The School of Peter Abelard: The Influence of Abelard's in the Early Scholastic Period*. Cambridge, 1969.

Weingart, R. E. *The Logic of Divine Love: A Critical Analysis of the Soteriology of Peter Abelard*. Oxford, 1979.

2 Bernard Silvester (d. ca. 1159)

Stock, B. *Myth and Science in the XIIth Century: A Study of Bernard Silvester*. Princeton, 1972.

3 Robert Grosseteste (fl. 1170–1253)

Callus, D. A. "The Oxford Career of Robert Grosseteste." *Oxoniensia* 10 (1945): 42–72.

Callus, D. A., ed. *Robert Grosseteste: Essays in Commemoration of the VIIth Century of his Death*. Oxford, 1955.

Crombie, A. C. *Robert Grosseteste and the Origins of Experimental Science*, Oxford, 1953.

Dunbabin, J. "Robert Grossteste as Translator, Transmitter and Commentator on the *Nicomachean Ethics*." *Traditio* 28 (1972): 460–472.

Southern, R. W. *Robert Grossteste: The Growth of an English Mind in Europe*. Oxford, 1986.

Thompson, S. H *The Writing of Robert Grossteste, Bishop of Lincoln, 1235–1253*. Cambridge, 1940.

4 Albert the Great (fl. 1200–1280)

Meyer, G. and A. Zimmerman, eds. *Albertus Magnus. Doctor Universalis*. Mayence, 1981.

5   *Roger Bacon (1214–1294)*

Easton, S. C. *Roger Bacon and the Search for a Universal Science*. Oxford, 1952.
Frankowska, M. *Scientia as Interpreted by Roger Bacon*. Varsovie, 1971.

6   *Bonaventure de Bagnoregio (fl. 1217–1274)*

Bettoni, E. *Saint Bonaventure*. Notre Dame, 1964.
Gilson, E. *The Philosophy of St. Bonaventura*. New York, 1938.

7   *Thomas Aquinas (1227–1274)*

Chenu, M. *Toward Understanding St. Thomas*. Chicago, 1964.
Coplestone, F. C. *Aquinas*. Baltimore, 1955.
Gilson, E. *The Philosophy of Thomas Aquinas*. 2nd edn, Cambridge, 1939.
Grabmann, M. *Thomas Aquinas*. New York, 1928.
Maritain, J. *Saint Thomas Aquinas*. London, 1931.
St. Thomas Aquinas, 1274–1974: Commemorative Studies. 2 vols. Toronto, 1974.

8   *Ramon Lull (1235–1315)*

Lohr, C. and F. Dominguez. "Raimundus Lullus, *Liber amici et amati:* Introduction and Critical Text." *Traditio* 44 (1988): 325–372.
Hillgarth, J. N. *Ramon Lull and Lullism in Fourteenth Century France*. Oxford, 1971.
Peers, E. A., ed. and trans. *Blanquerna: A Thirteenth-Century Romance Translated from the Catalan of Ramond Lull*. London, 1926.

9   *Siger de Brabant (1235–1281)*

F. van Steenberger, *Maître Siger de Brabant*. Louvain-Paris, 1977.

10   *Meister Eckhart (fl. 1260–1227?)*

Ancelet-Hustache, *Maître Eckhart et la Mystique rhénane*. Collection: "Maîtres spirituels". Paris, 1976.
Blakeney, R. B. *Meister Eckhart*. New York, 1941.
Clarke, J. M. *The Great German Mystics: Eckhart, Tauler and Suso*. Oxford, 1949.
Schurmann, Reiner, *Meister Eckhart, mystic and philosopher*. Bloomington, 1978.

11   Dante Alighieri (1265–1321)

Bergin, T. G. *Dante*. New York, 1965.

The Divine comedy and the Encyclopedia of arts and sciences. Acta of the International Dante Symposium, 13–16 November 1983, Hunter College, New York. ed. Giuseppe Di Scipio and A. Scaglione. Amsterdam-Philadelphia, 1988.

Ferrante, Joan M. *The political vision of the Divine comedy.* Princeton, 1984.

d'Entreves, A. P. *Dante as a Political Thinker,* London, 1952.

Gilbert, A. H. "Did Dante Dedicate the *Paradiso* to Can Grande?" *Italica* 42 (1966): 100–124.

Gilson, E. *Dante the Philosopher.* New York, 1949.

Hollander, R. *Allegory in Dante's commedia.* Princeton, 1969.

Mazzotta, G. *Dante, Poet of the Desert: History and Allegory in the Divine Comedy.* Princeton, 1979.

12   Duns Scotus (fl. 1270–1308)

Bettoni, E. *Duns Scotus.* Washington, D.C., 1961.

Harris, C. R. S. *Duns Scotus,* 2 vols. Oxford, 1927.

13   William of Ockham (fl. 1288–1348)

Boehner, P. *Collected Articles on Ockham.* New York, 1958.

Leff, G. *William of Ockham: The Metamorphoses of Scholastic Discourse.* Manchester, 1975.

Moody, A. A. *The Logic of William of Ockham.* New York, 1935.

Tornay, S. C. *Ockham: Studies and Selections.* LaSalle, ÍL, 1938.

14   John Wycliffe (1320?–1384)

Dahmus, J. *The Prosecution of John Wyclif.* New Haven, 1952.

Daly, L. J. *The Political Theory of John Wyclif.* Chicago, 1962.

MacFarlane, K. B. *John Wycliffe and the Beginnings of English Nonconformity.* London, 1952.

Robson, A. *Wyclif and the Oxford Schools.* Cambridge, 1966.

Workman, H. B. *John Wyclif.* 2 vols, Oxford, 1926.

15   Geoffrey Chaucer (fl. 1340–1400)

Bennet, H. S. *Chaucer and the Fifteenth Century.* Oxford, 1947.

Bennet, J. A. W. *Chaucer at Oxford and at Cambridge.* Toronto and Buffalo, 1974.

Brewer, D. S. *Chaucer in His Time*. London, 1963.
Donaldson, E. T. *Speaking of Chaucer*. New York, 1970.
Howard, D. R. *Chaucer: His Life, His Works, His World*. New York, 1987.
Jordan, R. M. *Chaucer and the Sape of Creation*. Cambridge, 1967.
Kolve, V. A., *Chaucer and the Imagery of Narrative: The First Five Canterbury Tales* (Stanford, Calif.: Stanford University Press, 1984).
Loomis, R. S. *A Mirror of Chaucer's World*. Princeton, 1965.
Marchette, Chute. *Geoffery Chaucer of England*. New York, 1946.
Robertson, D. W. *A Preface to Chaucer: Studies in Medieval Perspectives*. Princeton, 1962.

16   Jean Gerson (1363–1429)

Figgis, J. N. *From Gerson to Grotius*. 2nd edn, Cambridge, 1916.
Morrall, J. B. *Gerson and the Great Schism*. Manchester, 1961.
Ozment, S. E. "The University and the Church: Patterns of Reform in Jean Gerson. *Medievalia et Humanistica* n.s. 1 (1970): 111–126.

17   Nicholas of Cusa (1401–1464)

Sigmund, P. *Nicholas of Cusa*. Cambridge, MA, 1963.
Wantanabe, M. *The Political Ideas of Nicholas of Cusa*. Geneva, 1963.

18   Gabriel Biel (d. 1495)

Oberman, H. *The Harvest of Medieval Theology: Gabriel Biel and Late Medieval Nominalism*. Cambridge, MA, 1963.

INDEX